Poor Law Records
for
Family Historians

Simon Fowler

Published by
The Family History Partnership
PO Box 502
Bury, Lancashire BL8 9EP

Webpage: www.familyhistorypartnership.co.uk
Email: sales@thefamilyhistorypartnership.com

ISBN: 978 1 906280 29 1

First published 2011

Printed and bound by
Information Press, Southfield Road, Eynsham
Oxford OX29 4JB

Contents

Acknowledgements

Thanks to Bob Boyd, Richard Ratcliffe and Terry Walsh and the team at Family History Partnerhip for commissioning and publishing this title. Any errors or omissions are of course my own.

Preface

One of the rules of family history is that it is generally possible to find out more about the very rich and the very poor than any other group in society with the exception of service personnel, because more records were created for and about them. This guide looks at the poorest in society who were cared for (and often harrassed) by parish and poor law officials. And as money was involved, so records were kept.

Poor Law records are voluminous. That's the good news! The bad news is that their survival is patchy. Many were lost during various paper drives during the two world wars, eaten by vermin in parish chests or destroyed before their value to family and local historians was appreciated.

This guide offers an introduction to the records and how to use them if you are researching your pauper ancestors. With the exception of London surprisingly little is online, although this will change over the next few years, so you are likely to visit the archives in person to use the records.

Over the centuries, the Poor Law became a bureaucratic nightmare, but the records themselves are generally easy to use and can be surprisingly informative. There are two distinctive systems – the Old Poor Law which began in 1601 and the New Poor Law which took over in 1834. In addition there was a network of charities which helped those in temporary need. Again they left records which can prove useful, particularly for children.

How can I tell whether my ancestor was a pauper?

Being poor has always had a certain stigma attached. It is not something to which people like to admit. It is possible however that there may be family stories about being admitted to the workhouse or very occasionally, settlement certificates and related documents may turn up in family papers.

Old Poor Law (before 1834)
Many people realise that they have paupers in the family, when they find an entry in a parish register for an ancestor which indicates that the individual was a pauper. It might also be worth checking if you have an ancestor who lived to a great age, say over sixty, as they may well have received a small pension, often called 'out-relief, from the authorities. Single mothers and their children are also likely to have records about them. Between about 1810 and 1834, labourers and their families living in rural parishes in Southern England may well have received some support as well.

New Poor Law (after 1834)
You may be able to identify paupers from descriptions on birth and death certificates and entries in census enumerators' books. Death certificates will also note whether a person died in the workhouse. If a person was very old when he or she died, and came from a poor background, it is quite likely that she was admitted to the workhouse, particularly in the decades after 1850. Similarly many single mothers gave birth to illegitimate children in the workhouse, as they were one of the few places which admitted 'fallen' women and their babies.

In order to reduce the stigma, in 1911, the Registrar-General decreed that the workhouse could no longer be given as the place of birth or death. The guardians were forced to rename their institutions, and generally chose an odyne names. The one at Gressenhall became New Beech House. Bishop's Stortford was renamed Haymeads. However, these new titles were rarely used in other official documents.

General genealogical resources

The basic genealogical sources may sometimes provide clues or additional information about pauper ancestors so they should not be neglected.

Birth, Marriage and Death Records

Entries on birth, marriage and death certificates are often the first ways by which people become aware that they have pauper ancestors. For example, where no father's name is shown on the certificate, the birth was illegitimate. Illegitimacy rates declined during the nineteenth century from a high of about 7 per cent in the 1850s to 4 per cent in the 1890s. Many illegitimate births took place in workhouse infirmaries, so it is worth checking workhouse registers of births (if they survive) at the appropriate local record office to see whether the birth you are interested in appears there.

Alternatively, if the place of birth is shown as 'union workhouse' or something similar, again it is worth seeing whether the workhouse registers survive.

If the workhouse is indicated as place of death, or the workhouse master or matron is the person who reported the event, it is worth seeing whether there are registers of admission or death for the particular workhouse at the appropriate local record office. What records survive are listed in Jeremy Gibson's booklets on Poor Law Unions [see Select Bibliography] or may be listed on the record office's website.

A further complication is that in large cities there may be two or more workhouses with different names. So in Hull, for example, you need to be aware that Sculcoates was the Poor Law Union for the northern and eastern parts of the city. Again in Liverpool the West Derby Union covered the city's eastern suburbs.

Census Returns

It is fairly easy to identify paupers in census returns. For people receiving out-relief the entry in the occupations column may read something like 'pauper', 'on the parish' or 'on relief'. However, individuals noted as 'annuitants' are likely to be in receipt of a private pension. Workhouse masters and other employees of poor law unions are also likely to be identified as such. Workhouses, workhouse schools, county lunatic asylums, almshouses and the like appear in the census in the normal way. Sometimes individuals are named, but it is more common (frustratingly) just to find initials. This was a primitive – and effective – way of guaranteeing anonymity for the inmates.

Even so it may sometimes be possible to identify a person if he had unusual initials and you know his age, occupation or place of birth.

The online census indexes make it easy to find individuals, but it is more difficult to find the returns for a particular workhouse or orphanage. However, you can search by place on Findmypast (but not Ancestry), although you may need to know the street on which the workhouse was located.

- **www.findmypast.co.uk**

Although the 1911 census was released in 2009 a few entries were kept back over concerns for personal sensitivity. In particular details of babies born in workhouses were blanked out. However, all will be revealed on 1 January 2012.

Newspapers

Newspapers are another important – and under used resource – for studying the Poor Law, particularly the New Poor Law. It is unlikely however that individual paupers will be mentioned, although the appointment and the resignation or dismissal of officials might well be. In local newspapers you are likely to find almost verbatim accounts of the meetings of the Boards of Guardians, and the occasional account of a visit made by a reporter to the local workhouse. Local newspapers are also likely to include in great detail, debates about the treatment of the paupers, especially on such minor issues as whether inmates should be allowed beer with their Christmas dinner. I've even come across the inclusion of applications for jobs together with references.

National newspapers also took a keen interest in the Poor Law, particularly in the 1830s and 1840s. *The Times,* for example, was prominent in exposing the Andover Workhouse Scandal. [See pages 28 and 34].

Local newspapers are generally to be found in record offices or in local studies libraries. They are almost always produced on microfilm which can be quite tiring to use. Rarely are they indexed to any great degree, so you will need to know roughly when the event you are interested took place. On the other hand many local studies libraries maintain large and well-indexed collections of press cuttings which are generally easier to use.

The national collection of newspapers at the British Library Newspapers Library at Colindale in North London holds over 50,000 different titles dating back to the end of the 17th century. Its catalogue is at **http://catalogue.bl.uk**. Colindale will be closing by 2012 and the collection is moving to the British Library Centre at Boston Spa near Leeds. An increasing number of papers for the nineteenth century are being digitised. At present, more than 50 newspapers and magazines published between 1800 and 1899 have been digitised including many local papers. More will be added over the next few years.

- **http://newspapers.bl.uk**

If you are lucky your local library may subscribe to this pay per view site so you can access it there for free, otherwise you have to pay for access. At the time of writing it costs £6.99 for a day's access or £9.99 for seven days. It's easy to search by name or place. You can do a preliminary search for free. The short extracts contain just enough information to confirm whether the story is about your ancestor or not.

Many libraries (including The National Archives) also provide access to The Times Digital Archive with digitised images of each article and a comprehensive index. Again you may be able to access this at home if your local library provides the service. Check your council's website.

The Old Poor Law

Before 1834 the very poorest in society were cared for by the parish in which they lived or had right of settlement. During medieval times it was the duty of the church to care for the poor as had been laid down in the scriptures, especially in the Acts of Corporal Mercy. Following the dissolution of the monasteries, the Reformation led to a succession of ineffectual, and cruel laws. The Poor Law Act of 1547, for example, allowed branding and slavery as the punishments for persistent vagrancy. Another of 1572 ordered beggars to be branded on the shoulder. Meanwhile the parish and private charities were left to cope with the elderly and the chronically sick who were the people most in need of help.

Eventually Parliament took effective action with the Poor Law Act of 1601 – often called the '43rd Elizabeth', after the regnal year in which it was passed. This legislation was the basis of the Old Poor Law until it crumpled under the great pressures on society unleashed by the Industrial Revolution. Each parish was to elect two or three substantial householders each year to be Overseers of the Poor who were made responsible for providing work for the unemployed and provide relief for the lame, the impotent, the old, blind and others being poor and not able to work, the funds being provided by a levy of a poor rate on the inhabitants. The 1601 Act was amended in 1662 establishing rights of settlement.

Settlement was granted to people who were either born in a parish, or had rented property, paid the poor rate, or had lived for a period of one year in their new parish of residence. If they could not prove their right of settlement when they sought help they were liable to be sent back to the parish of their birth. Paupers were given certificates from their parish of settlement guaranteeing to receive them back if they sought assistance.

During the seventeenth, and especially during the eighteenth century, many parishes established workhouses to house paupers. The intention was to reduce the cost of the poor rate, by forcing all those in receipt of assistance to live together. In Beverley a new workhouse opened in 1727 capable of housing a hundred people. A year later the overseers reported that they had given

"... notice to all the Poor that the Weekly Allowances were to cease at Midsummer, that such as were not able to maintain themselves and their families must apply to the governors of the workhouse to be by them provided for. And though before the opening of the [work]house 116 received the parish allowance, not above 8 came in at first and we have never exceeded 26 in the house all this winter, though all kinds of provisions have been very dear and the season very sickly..."

They felt that had the house not been opened they "would have had not less than 200 people upon their hands."

Not every parish established a workhouse, and in many places the poor, especially the elderly and infirm, were well treated. It was clearly better for the elderly to be looked after by family and neighbours in their own homes, rather than to be admitted to an institution where board and lodging had to be met from the poor rate. Overseers' Accounts are full of such payments. The accounts for Aspley Guise, Bedfordshire in 1759 contain the following entries:

19 January 1759: paid for a broth of mutton for Mary Axham being sick	9d
21 February 1759: paid for 2lb of mutton for Widow Dounton being sick	7d
March 1759: paid for wood for Widow Houghton	5s
10 March 1759: paid Mary Bushby for nursing Widow Doulton	1s
10 March 1759: paid Mary Batterham for nursing Mary Axham being sick	3s
May 1759: to Widow Duncombe's boy a rushy drabb and thread for a pair of breeches for making ditto	6s 2d

Although conditions in workhouses were meant to be a deterrent, many parishes took great pride in maintaining a welcoming home for their elderly and infirm. The Royal Commission on the Poor Law, which took evidence between 1832 and 1834, praised the workhouse in Richmond in Surrey. There the inspector, Charles Maclean, found "as a building the house has many advantages, but the interior arrangement which depends on the governor and the appearance of the inmates is extremely creditable to him."

Further down the Thames Valley in Reading another inspector, Edwin Chadwick, praised the quality of the beer at the house maintained by the parish of St Lawrence remarking that it "tasted excellent."

As each parish took care of its own, the quality of assistance offered could vary tremendously. In part this might depend on local circumstances. A relatively unpopulated and prosperous rural parish, such as Apsley Guise, might have very few elderly persons or paupers to look after. A few miles away the position could be very different for a parish in the heart of a town , such as Bedford, which might have to care for many hundreds of paupers in its overcrowded streets.

Another factor was the interest shown by the Overseers of the Poor, who were elected each year by the ratepayers. It was a thankless and unpaid duty in which few men outside the clergy had any particular interest. They were often local farmers, in rural parishes, and shopkeepers and merchants in the towns all with a keen desire to keep expenditure as low as possible.

A lot also depended on the quality of the officials running the workhouse or paying pensions to widows. Their experience and ability varied greatly and this would have an impact on the provision made for the poor. Richmond, with its affluent population of concerned citizens, long had a reputation for the efficient administration of the Poor Law. Charles Maclean thought that their example could be adopted "with advantage" by other parishes. Across the river in Brentford, however the position was very different. Here the Poor Law was renowned for its corruption and inefficiency, for the same family ran the local workhouse for many years.

Although not perfect the Poor Law system worked reasonably well in a stable largely agrarian society where the population growth was low or nonexistent. By the 1780s and 1790s this was no longer the case. Population growth and industrialisation was beginning to impose enormous strains on the Poor Law system as more and more people sought relief to tide them and their families over. The amount paid in poor law relief rose from £3m in 1783 to some £7m in 1820.

The reasons for this increase are clear. In particular, the population was growing rapidly, increasing during the eighteenth century from about 5.5m in 1700 to 8.9m in 1801. By 1831 it had reached nearly 14m.

The Industrial Revolution drew in people to the new industrial areas of the West Midlands and the North. Agriculture too was changing with new methods and machinery reducing the need for labour. Twenty years of war with France from 1793 cut trade with the Continent and led to considerable unemployment.

Economic conditions hardly improved in the twenty years after Waterloo with more unemployment in rural and some industrial areas.

The crisis particularly affected rural parishes in the South of England. One solution adopted in many places was to use the poor rate to make up labourers' wages. The first parish to adopt this was Speenhamland in Berkshire in 1795 where the Overseers of the Poor agreed to supplement low wages with an allowance paid from the poor rates. The Speenhamland System was widely adopted across the whole of Southern England. An alternative was to assign unemployed labourers to farmers whether they needed extra labour or not, part of whose wages was met by the parish and part by the farmer himself.

Although adopted with the best of intentions these solutions to rural unemployment actually added to the problem. Because local farmers often deliberately kept wages low, in the expectation that allowances would be given by the parish, the number of people on poor relief actually rose. Those who had men assigned to them found it difficult to support them. This was a constant source of complaint to the Royal Commission on the Poor Law. In Frensham, Surrey, William Mayhew told the assistant commissioner:

> "I have sons (eight) enough to do the whole work on my farm (about sixty acres) and to be compelled to pay for labour, the consequences would be, I must bring up my own children in idleness to employ and pay others; and in that case it must be injurious; ... it is impossible in the present state of things for ... man to live and pay his way."

Eventually it became clear that the old system could no longer cope - that it was making idle tens of thousands who would rather work and it was not directing assistance to where it was most needed. A Royal Commission was appointed in February 1832 to investigate and make recommendations. It reported two years later having undertaken a massive survey of the current position. It proposed a major overhaul of the Poor Law by establishing Poor Law Unions - groups of parishes which would run workhouses where all paupers would be housed. The proposals were especially harsh on the poor, for it severely limited the support they could expect from the authorities.

The Records of the Old Poor Law

Almost all the records described below are to be found at County Record Offices. Their survival however is patchy. So, it is a very good idea to contact the record office in advance before you set out. Those for Inner London are being digitised and placed online by Ancestry (**www.ancestry.co.uk/London**), but relatively little else is yet available on the internet. It is also worth seeing if local family history societies have produced indexes to some of the records. These may be available in local libraries and archives or can be purchased from the societies themselves. The Society of Genealogists in London may also have copies in their library.

Settlement and Removal

Records of settlement are probably the most interesting and useful records for family historians. They bring into sharp focus the meeting point between the poor and the system of relief. In the case of settlement examinations, although they record who was entitled to relief from which parish, they offer a vivid insight into eighteenth century life and the lives of the very poorest in particular.

- The 1662 Settlement Law allowed for the removal of people claiming relief who did not have the right to reside (that is legal settlement) in a particular place. Right of settlement was granted under various circumstances:
- A legitimate child took his father's settlement, which may not be same as where the child was born.
- A wife took her husband's settlement
- A widow who remarried took her husband's settlement. Children from her first marriage retained their father's settlement.
- Children from the age of seven and upwards could gain settlement in the parish where they were apprenticed, providing they lived there for more than forty consecutive days.
- Servants who stayed one year from date of hiring, and left with full wages, could claim settlement in the place where they were in service.
- A married man who rented a farm or smallholding, or set up as a tradesman in a new parish, providing he stayed twelve months, paid parish rates and £10 or more in annual rent, could gain a new settlement there.
- A person who inherited an estate of land and lived on the estate for more than forty days could claim a settlement there.

Individuals claiming settlement had to prove this in front of two or more Justices of the Peace (magistrates) who would sign the examination together with the claimant. The person seeking settlement would be keen to stress their history of employment, often citing individual masters or mistresses, as well as their place of birth and parishes in which they had lived. For a man

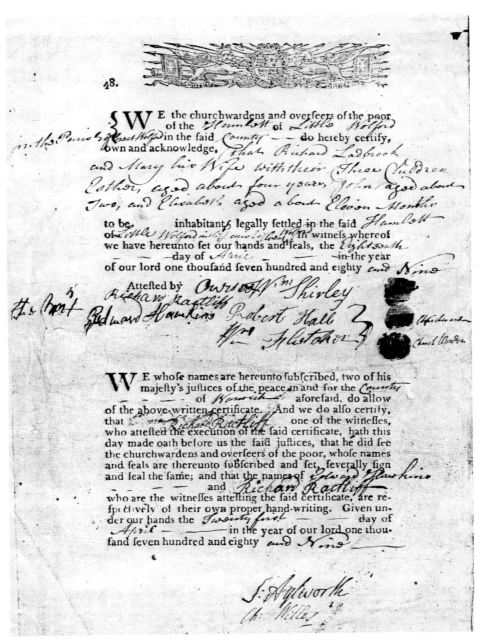

Settlement certificate for Richard Ladbrook and his family at Great Wolford, Warwickshire in 1789. (Ref. Warwickshire CRO DR81/29)

Settlement examination for John Podmore, aged 33 years, resident in the parish of Lilleshall, John Podmore was born and worked in Tibberton in the Edgemore Parish. He had a wife, Mary and 6 children. The settlement is dated 20th May 1811. (Shropshire Archives reference P161/L/5/13) claiming settlement, details of spouse and children are sometimes given. The information given does vary however. A typical example is:

"George Bradly, aged about 37 years upon oath saith that he was born in that part of the royal parish at Kensington which is in the parish of St Margaret Westminster...And saith that the late Dr Richard Bradly, a professor of botany was this examinant's father and that he rented a house of about £7 a year about 25 years ago at North End in the Parish of Fulham... about the space of seven years and paid all parochial taxes for the same. And that examinant lived with his said father at the same time... he had not been an apprentice, or rented a house of £10 a year, or paid any parochial taxes or done any act or thing (to the best of his knowledge) to gain a settlement. And saith that in the month of February 1731 he... was married to Mary, his present wife at the parish church of St Clement Danes... by whom he has three children living... Mary about 10 years, Lucy about 7 years and George about 5 years. Sworn 22 June 1742.

Source: Tim Hitchcock and John Black (eds), *Chelsea Settlement and Bastardy Examinations, 1733-1766* (London Record Society, 1999) No. 110

A number of settlement examinations have been transcribed and published by local family history or county record societies, so it is always worth enquiring whether this has happened for the parish in which you are interested.

Also worth looking out for are Settlement Certificates which were given to paupers as proof of legal settlement in a parish. The information given in these certificates varies, but can include details not just of the individual himself, but his family as well. Like all poor law records their survival is patchy. Occasionally they may be part of a collection of family papers, but more often they can be found in the parish papers relating to poor relief at county record offices.

Removal Orders returning paupers back to their parish of settlement are another useful source. As two copies of the order were made for each parish involved, their survival rate is relatively good. Late eighteenth and nineteenth century orders can be particularly informative giving reasons for the person's removal and other details of a family's circumstances, for example whether the father was in prison or whether a woman was pregnant.

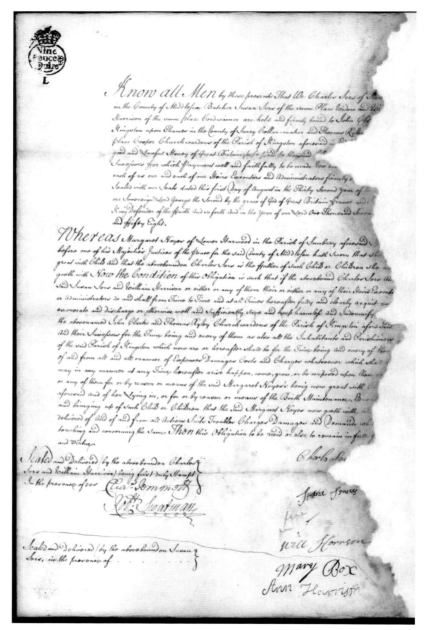

An example of a removal order issued in 1783. (Royal Borough of Kingston-upon-Thames Document reference KG 3/5/1)

There are however many oddities and exceptions – e.g. the parish of Stepney in London's East End and the heart of the city's docks. Because of the great numbers of sailors living there in the seventeenth and eighteenth centuries, it became a favourite place for parishes from all over the country to offload paupers who were, or claimed to have been, born at sea. If a parish constable found a vagrant sailor wandering the streets of Liverpool or Bristol, he might get sent off to Stepney.

Bastardy Orders

Parish authorities were also responsible for the maintenance of single mothers and their bastard children. Much time was spent seeking the reputed father and either making him marry the unfortunate woman or assume responsibility for her maintenance.

Once an Overseer of the Poor knew who the father of a bastard child was, he would obtain a Bastardy Bond drawn up by a Justice of the Peace, which was an agreement between the man and the parish to pay costs relating to the child. On the birth of the child a maintenance order was made in which the man was ordered to pay a named sum, being the costs of birth, plus one shilling and sixpence a week for maintenance of the child. Many men accused of fathering a child naturally tried to run away, so the Overseers would obtain a Bastardy Warrant to track him down and force him to pay towards the upkeep of his child.

The information contained on these records varies depending on the circumstances and the diligence of local officials, but you should be able to find more about the father and his occupation, and the date and place of birth of the child.

Even after 1834 the authorities still made considerable attempts to identify the fathers of bastard children. There may be material in the Poor Law Union records, particularly the minutes of the Boards of Guardians. There may also be orders for maintenance under the Bastardy Act 1845.

Examinations were made by the magistrates in order to identify the father who would be charged with maintaining the bastard child. Here again they represent the voice of the poor – the prostitute and the destitute - who rarely feature in the written record. They can be a very valuable source, as they are full of information unobtainable elsewhere:

> The voluntary examination of Dorothy Fielding widow taken upon oath us… who says that on 31 Dec last [1748] she… was delivered of a female bastard child … in the parish of Great Chelsea…(which child is

baptised and named Mary). And was unlawfully begotten on her body by one Richard Vincent the elder, a musician living at the Turks Head and Cock in Bedford Street in the parish of St Paul's Covent Garden… Who had carnal knowledge of her body the first time in the dwelling house of Mrs Thorogood on Panton Fields near Leicester Fields and several times in the said house and other places. And this examinant also says that the said Richard Vincent is the true father of the said child…. Sworn, 27 June 1749 before us Peter Elers, Thomas Ellys.
Source: *Chelsea Settlement and Bastardy Examinations, 1733-1766*, No. 210.

Parish Records
Each of the 15,000 or so parishes in England and Wales annually had to appoint Overseers of the Poor. The overseers themselves created many records, of which the most important are probably the accounts, which record every penny spent by them in the course of their duties. From the accounts one can get a pretty good idea of the scope of the overseers' work, whether it was the payment of pensions to widows and widowers, the amount spent on removing a pauper to another parish, or the purchase of items of clothing for orphans. Although sometimes difficult to read these accounts are full of human detail and may well mention grants and gifts made to your ancestors.

The overseers were responsible to the Parish Vestry which discussed and approved the action of their officers. Where they survive Vestry Minutes may record why payments were made to a pauper ancestor and the result of their actions.

Another important administrative body was the Quarter Sessions. Paupers threatened with removal or unhappy with their treatment could appeal to the Quarter Sessions. The Sessions were particularly opposed to vagrants, rogues and vagabonds who were perceived as being a threat to the peace. Quarter Sessions papers often include Examinations of these people, who were for the most part men and women tramping the country seeking work when some misfortune befell them and they were forced to seek help. Vagrants were examined and orders were issued for removal to their place of settlement. The records can give you some idea of where they were sent, as well as their personal circumstances. As the numbers on the tramp increased dramatically after the end of the Napoleonic Wars the system gradually fell into disuse, which may explain why there is relatively little material after 1820.

The survival of Quarter Sessions records is very patchy. Cambridgeshire Quarter Sessions records, for example, are almost non-existent, whereas most survive for Surrey. They can be difficult to use, often written in Latin before 1733 and the judgements themselves hard to read. A useful introduction to these records is Jeremy Gibson's *Quarter Sessions Records for Family Historians* (Family History Partnership). Full catalogues exist online at **www.nationalarchives.gov.uk/a2a**.

Apprenticeship Records

Poor children, especially those who were maintained by the parish, could be apprenticed to local traders and shopkeepers. Copies of pauper apprentice-ship documents or indentures are often to be found in parish records. They give the name of the child and the person to whom he or she was being ap-prenticed. The trade to be taught is often given.

The apprenticing of individual children is usually recorded in the Vestry Minute books or in the overseer's accounts.

After 1834, much greater care was taken when children were apprenticed. Guardians often inspected the places where children were to be sent, and this may be recorded in the minutes of the Boards of Guardians. There may also be registers of apprentices and copies of indentures and other records ac-companying the minute books.

Royal Commission on the Poor Law

The Commissioners sent a number of assistants round the country in 1832 and 1833 to see what the position was locally. They visited about a fifth of all parishes in England and Wales. Overseers or poor law officials were asked to complete a questionnaire about provisions made for poor relief in their parish. The completion of this questionnaire was patchy, as only a fifth of parishes bothered to return it.

Although sketchy this evidence offers a unique view of the lives of poor people in the early 1830s. The commissioners spoke to many labourers and their views are recorded verbatim in the records. In addition they include in-formation about many individual paupers. In Thurgarton in Nottinghamshire, they describe all the labourers in the village, for example:

> Robert Barker. 11 children born, 7 living. Rent of cottage and garden £1 1s. £35 11s 6d in savings bank. 10s a week earnings increased to 12s in harvest. Has one daughter [at home] grown up, almost an idiot.

The records of the Commissioners can be found in the published Parliamentary Papers to be found in some large libraries and most university libraries. The verbatim accounts of interviews with, and other records, of paupers are mainly found in Appendix A of these papers.

The New Poor Law

Origin

During the early decades of the nineteenth century it was increasingly clear that the old poor law could not cope with the rising number of paupers. The poor rate, which paid for their care, was an increasing burden on middle-class pockets. Spending on the poor law rose from about £4m in 1800 to £7m by 1830. This rise in pauperism was largely the result of dislocation caused by the agricultural and industrial revolutions and the aftermath of the Napoleonic Wars. Rural and semi-rural areas were particularly badly affected. This was coupled with a growing sentiment that the real enemy was not poverty, but pauperism – a character defect involving idleness, unreliability and above all drunkenness, which threatened the stability and respectability of society.

In 1832 the government set up the Royal Commission on the Poor Law to investigate the situation. Its report, which was largely enacted as the Poor Law (Amendment) Act 1834, had a simple solution to the problem. Outdoor relief was to be phased out. Everybody who applied for relief would be offered the workhouse in which their lives would be regulated and made less comfortable than those who decided to stay outside the poor law and fend for themselves. Only those who were in the direst need would accept the workhouse.

The Commission's report was flawed in that it did not understand the root causes of pauperism. It concluded from the partial evidence before it that it was easy for men whose relief was withdrawn to obtain other work, finding that: "One of the most encouraging of the results of our inquiry is the degree to which the existing pauperism arises from fraud, indolence or improvidence." Most of the able-bodied men and women who sought relief were the victims of unemployment or low wages rather than workshy layabouts.

The new Act met with stiff resistance particularly in East Anglia and the North, where considerable protests were mounted against the 'Pauper's Bastille' as the protesters called the workhouses. Even a decade after the introduction of the New Poor Law *The Times* reported outbreaks of the burning of ricks and other property belonging to farmers in Norfolk and Suffolk, which its correspondent attributed to the workhouse. He asked a labourer what was the cause of the fires, who replied: "If there had been no union, in my opinion there would have been no fires, and everybody says the same that I hear. The union distresses people and drives them mad."

The first Poor Law Unions were formed in southern England during 1835. But it was not until 1837 and 1838 that unions began to appear in the industrial North. In a few places workhouses were not provided until the 1870s. The last was in Todmorden in Lancashire which finally opened in 1877.

Organisation

The basic administrative units of the New Poor Law were the Poor Law Union, of which around 650 were eventually created throughout England and Wales. These unions were responsible for the implementation of the Poor Law locally. Unions might include parishes from several different counties. Some boundaries were changed over time and parishes were transferred from one union to another. Full details are given in Jeremy Gibson's *Poor Law Union Records* or online at **www.workhouses.org.uk**.

Each Poor Law Union was run by an elected Board of Guardians. The guardians were elected annually by local ratepayers, although magistrates were also ex-officio members. The guardians were a mixture of local gentry, and small businessmen. One of the constant complaints made about the administration of unions was the penny-pinching way in which the guardians carried out their work, which critics blamed on the number of shopkeepers on the board who were determined to keep the rates down rather than improve conditions in the workhouse. During the 1880s a small number of women and from the 1890s working class men, began to be elected as guardians. On the whole these new faces brought a breath of welcome humanity and common sense to the workhouse.

One of the most effective of the new breed of guardian was George Lansbury who was elected to the board at Poplar in East London. He later wrote:

"My first visit to a workhouse, was a memorable one. Going down the narrow lane, ringing the bell, waiting while an official with a not too pleasant face looked through a grating to see who was there, and hearing his unpleasant voice—of course, he did not know me—made it easy for me to understand why the poor dreaded and hated these places, and made me in a flash realise how all these prison or bastille sort of surroundings were organised for the purpose of making self-respecting, decent people endure any suffering rather than enter. It was not necessary to write up the words 'Abandon hope all ye who enter here'."

The formal business of the guardians was discussed at the board meeting which was normally held weekly. In smaller unions the board might well discuss the admission and discharge of individual paupers and any punishment meted out to them. Over time in most unions a system of committees grew up which oversaw aspects of the work. They might include boarding-out (supervising children placed with local families), dispensary, finance, general purpose, house (supervising the workhouse), stores, and women's committees.

In addition the guardians had other responsibilities including the administration of the registration of births, marriages and deaths (before 1871), inoculation of babies with smallpox vaccine and some public health duties.

But most of their work was concerned with caring for the local poor. They had two very blunt tools at their disposal - indoor and outdoor relief. Indoor relief meant "offering" the applicant the workhouse.

Outdoor, or out-relief, involved the payment of small sums to the sick and the elderly who were not admitted to the workhouse. Under the 1834 legislation out-relief was meant to be phased out, but all but a few unions continued to pay it, although to a lesser degree than had previously been the case. By the end of the nineteenth century three-quarters of all paupers received out-relief. Guardians realised that it cost less and was more humane.

Each union maintained at least one workhouse. In addition there might also be a school and an infirmary for inmates. Particularly in the London area unions might co-operate to run a school or an asylum.

The most important official was the Workhouse Master, often assisted by his wife as the Workhouse Matron. In the early years, at least, they might run the house single-handed. In 1834, the master and his wife at the Southwell Workhouse in Nottinghamshire looked after 158 paupers.

Another important official was the Relieving Officer, responsible for admitting paupers to the workhouse and dealing with out-relief. Unions also employed clerks to the guardians, treasurers, medical officers, schoolmasters and mistresses, and chaplains. In the smaller unions these people might well be local solicitors, general practitioners, and clergymen who received a small stipend in return for services rendered.

The splendid façade of Gressingham House of Industry opened in 1776 to house and employ paupers from 58 parishes in mid-Norfolk.

Poor Law Unions received advice, and a modicum of direction, from White-hall in the form of the Poor Law Commissoners between 1834 and 1847, Poor Law Board (1848-1871), Local Government Board (1871-1918), and Ministry of Health (1919-1929). In addition a number of poor law inspectors (origi-nally assistant poor law commissioners) constantly visited workhouses to ensure that minimum standards were met, while district auditors combed the accounts in search of unauthorised or irregular expenditure. The reports of the inspectorate can be very illuminating about workhouses and conditions of the poor locally, although names of individuals are very rarely to be found. The Poor Law was paid for by a rate levied on ratepayers. Before 1862 this was collected by individual parishes, thereafter it was assessed and collected by the union, except in London where it was the responsibility of the Metro-politan Common Poor Fund.

The Workhouse
With the establishment of Poor Law Unions in 1834, parochial workhouses were closed down often to be replaced by a purpose built central building – three hundred new workhouses were built in the decade after the establish-ment of poor law unions.

Life in the workhouse consisted of any number of petty humiliations. In particular men and women were kept separate. Indeed there was a further division into those who were thought capable of work "able-bodied paupers" and those who could not. Families were broken up and children, except ba-bies, were taken from their mothers. People slept in draughty dormitories – generally called wards. There was a work yard where paupers would earn their keep by breaking stones and picking oakum. The worst conditions were found in the casual wards, which housed vagrants tramping the country look-ing for work.

For most paupers and their masters a matter of crucial importance was food and drink. The authorities in Whitehall laid down a "dietary" which workhouses had to follow, although some local discretion was permitted. For example in 1869, the Poor Law Board recommended that able-bodied paupers should have for breakfast 7 ounces of bread, and 1.5 pints of por-ridge. The diet was just about adequate but desperately dull. At Christmas, and national celebrations such as Queen Victoria's Diamond Jubilee, however, inmates were regularly treated to roast beef and perhaps a mug of beer.

The workhouses soon got the reputation, of being cruel and heartless places. During the 1840s, there were a number of scandals about conditions in workhouses. The worst of these was at Andover. Here conditions were so bad that during 1846 paupers were reduced to eating the marrow from the bones for sustenance they were supposed to be crushing. In 1848, 180 children died as a result of a cholera outbreak at Drouet's School in Tooting where many London unions had sent their children. Charles Dickens' view was shared by many that "Mr Drouet's farm for children... was brutally conducted, vilely kept, preposterously inspected, dishonestly defended, a disgrace to a Christian community, and a stain upon a civilised land."

After the 1850s workhouses increasingly became the refuge of outcasts from society. As early as 1852, Robert Pashley wrote: "Each building which we absurdly call a workhouse is in truth a general hospital, an almshouse, an idiot house, a blind asylum, a deaf and dumb asylum...and a workhouse. But this last part of the establishment omits to find work even for the able-bodies." Residents overwhelmingly consisted of the elderly, orphans, nursing mothers with bastard children, and the insane. A survey in 1897 found that a third of old people over seventy were helped in some way by the poor law authorities.

In the second half of the nineteenth century conditions slowly began to improve. Particular attention was paid to the schooling of children in the home in the hope that they would not follow their parents' example, and, in many unions from the 1880s, they were raised in cottage homes away from the regimented life of the workhouse. In small ways too, life in the workhouse got better, especially for the elderly. Old couples were allowed to see each other during the day and the diet improved.

Despite these changes the workhouse was increasingly seen as being outdated by the beginning of the twentieth century. The government set up a Royal Commission in November 1905 to investigate the Poor Law and make recommendations for its reform. It recommended the abolition of the Poor Law Unions and the passing of their duties to local government.

It wasn't until 1929 however that guardians were abolished and their duties taken over by local councils. Most workhouses became hospitals or homes for elderly; indeed a few still remain in use, but they have largely been demolished. The Poor Law however was not finally abolished until 1948 when the Welfare State was introduced.

Records of the New Poor Law

Records of the New Poor Law are split between The National Archives (TNA) and local record offices. Material relating to the day to day operations of individual poor law unions are generally to be found locally, while TNA has

Inmates in the Aged Female Ward at Gateshead Workhouse, 1896. By this time conditions particularly for the elderly had improved. (Gateshead Metropolitan Borough)

documents on relations with the Poor Law Commissioners and their successors.

The National Archives

The major source is the correspondence between the Poor Law Commissioners and individual unions in series MH 12. These records begin in 1834 and finish about 1900. Most later records were destroyed in the Blitz. What little survives is in MH 68.

They contain considerable correspondence about the workhouse, particularly at times when building work was planned to expand or improve the house. This material can give a vivid idea of what it must have been like to have been a resident of the workhouse. Incidentally, series MH 14 contains plans of lands and buildings, listed alphabetically by union between 1861 and 1918.

Amongst this correspondence you may find returns to circulars sent out by the Commissioners. They include lists of people who had been vaccinated against smallpox in the union, paupers granted money to emigrate, and details of pauper lunatics and where they were looked after.

If the union ran a workhouse school the reports of the poor law inspectors include details about the quality of tuition and the abilities of the schoolmaster or mistress. A few unions ran joint school districts, particularly in London. Records of districts are in MH 27. They relate to the administration of and control of the schools, including the appointment of managers, teaching and nursing staff, inspection of schools, construction and financing of buildings and related medical services. MH 17 contains similar papers of the Sick Asylum Districts in London, and the Metropolitan Asylum Board.

Whitehall had to approve the appointment of staff employed by local unions. Correspondence can be found in MH 12, while registers of people employed by unions can be found in MH 9. They cover the period between 1837 and 1921, although the vast majority of entries are for the second half of the 19th century. The registers are arranged by union. They contain dates of appointments and salary awarded. Reasons for leaving employment are noted, if they were known.

Scattered through MH 12 are application forms from people seeking employment as workhouse master, teacher or medical officer. Initially these forms were introduced in 1842 for medical officers but were extended in the mid-1840s to other staff. There may also be letters from employees complaining about conditions or seeking pay rises.

Reports from poor law inspectors on conditions in workhouses and the problems faced by local boards of guardians are largely in MH 32, with some found in MH 12. The reports in MH 32 are generally arranged by name of inspector, which can be frustrating if you are looking for an individual union. From the 1870s specialist inspectors for buildings, infirmaries, and schools (including a few women) were increasingly recruited.

Unfortunately, the records can be difficult to use. In particular the correspondence in MH 12 is filed in tightly bound volumes whose bindings are gently disintegrating. There are no meaningful indexes. However, partial help is at hand in the form of the " Living the Poor Lives" project, which is transcribing and digitising correspondence from some 22 unions between 1834 and 1871. The detailed transcripts are in the main TNA catalogue and the digitised letters can be downloaded for free from Documents Online (**www.nationalarchives.gov.uk/documentsonline**). More information about the project can be found at **www.nationalarchives.gov.uk/about/living-poor-life.htm**.

Local Record Offices

Collections of Poor Law Union records at local record offices are very patchy. As a result it is not possible to give any clear idea of what might survive for a particular union or workhouse. On the other hand, many of the forms and registers completed by officials duplicate each other, so if one set of records has been lost another of similar type may be equally suitable.

A comprehensive list of what records survive for each union can be found in the three volumes of Jeremy Gibson's *Poor Law Union Records* (Family History Partnership). Brief details can also be found on the appropriate individual workhouse page at **www.workhouses.org.** Many records for workhouses and poor law unions in inner London are being digitised and indexed by Ancestry (**www.ancestry.co.uk/London**). The project is not complete at time of writing and it is hard to find out what has been digitised and what is waiting to be copied.

The most important series of records are:

- Minutes of the Board of Guardians and its various sub-committees. These may contain minutes about troublesome inmates or the apprenticing of individual children. You may occasionally find lists of paupers or, with the appropriate committee papers, lists of pauper children.
- Registers of indoor-relief personnel. These records come in various forms. For example registers of admission and discharges from the workhouse, or printed indoor relief lists which were published every six months. Not dissimilar are the creed registers which, from 1876, contain religious and other personal details about paupers.
- Registers of children, including admissions to the workhouse school. There may also be registers noting the employment of children or indicating where they were boarded-out.
- Registers of lunatics in asylums.
- Registers or books of paupers receiving out-relief. There may also be printed outdoor relief lists showing where every recipient lived and giving the reason why they received support. Also of considerable interest are application and report, or case, books in which details of applications for relief are given.

However, some of these records which are less than 75 years old and sometimes 100 years old may be closed to public access.

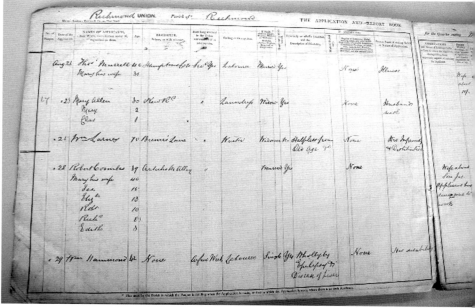

Entries in the minute book of the Board of Guardians, Richmond, 1888-1890. (Surrey History Centre BG 10/10/11/21)

Entries in a register of applicants for out-relief in Richmond, August 1873. (Surrey History Centre BG 10/55/3)

A LIST OF PERSONS

Who receive regular Weekly & Occasional Relief

FROM THE OVERSEERS

OF THE PARISH OF KINGSTON.

NAMES OF PAUPERS.	Age.	Number of Children Dependent.	Amount of Relief. s. d.	CAUSE OF RELIEF.	OBSERVATIONS.
Adams, John, and Wife ...	45	4	2 6	Family	*Surbiton Common.*
Arley, Judith	43	4	10 0	Husband left her	*Romsey, Hants.*
Andrew's, Widow, Child ..	—	—	2 6	Father dead	*Hampton Wick.*
Alexander and Wife	40	3	5 0	Family and little work	*Church Yard Row.*
Ayres, Richard, and Wife	40	6	5 0	Family and illness	*Surbiton Common.*
Arnot, Robert, and Wife ..	59	1	3 0	Infirm and illness	*Isleworth.*
** Barfoot, Elizabeth	38	2	3 0	Family	*Back Lanes.*
Baker, James, and Wife ...	33	4	5 0	Family	*Long Ditton.*
Barnes, Widow	73	—	2 6	Infirm	*Hanworth.*
Baton, William, and Wife	36	6	5 0	Family	*London Street.*
Barnes, Sarah	25	—	2 0	Infirm	*Harrow on the Hill.*
Baker, William	43	4	7 0	Family and illness	*Chertsey.*
Bembrick, William, & Wife	72	—	4 0	Infirm and ill	*Apple Market.*
Beck, Charlotte	34	—	2 6	Fits	*Thames Ditton.*
Benwell, William, and Wife	40	3	2 6	Family	*Hampton Wick.*
Beasmore, Widow	70	—	2 6	Infirm	*London Road.*
Bennett, William, and Wife	56	2	4 0	Family and illness	*Kensington.*
Beckford, Widow	76	—	3 0	Infirm	*Cheam.*
Berryman's Child	12	—	2 0	Orphan	*St. Nicholas, Abingdon.*
Bennett, Widow	61	—	2 0	Infirm	*Fulham.*
** Bignold, Henry, & Wife	38	8	5 0	Family	*Heathen Street.*
Billingham, Widow	62	—	3 0	Infirm	*Horse Fair.*
Blunden, Widow	62	1	2 6	Infirm	*London.*
Bonor and Wife	70	—	2 0	Infirm	*High Row.*
Bristow, Widow	46	4	9 0	Family	*Bittoms.*
Brown, Nelly, Widow	83	—	2 6	Infirm	*Back Lanes.*
Brown, Widow	43	2	4 0	Family, 1 child a cripple	*London Road.*
Bridget's Child	5	—	2 0	Father dead, illegitimate	*Croydon.*
Bradger, Widow	41	2	5 0	Family	*London.*
Brown's Child	4	—	2 0	Illegitimate	*London.*
Butler, Widow	84	—	2 0	Infirm	*London.*
Butler's Children	—	3	7 6	Father run away	*London Road.*
Bullen, Widow	40	2	6 0	Family	*Heathen Street.*
Busk, Widow	79	—	2 0	Infirm	*Horse Fair.*
Burton	61	—	2 6	Illness	*Thames Street.*
** Cager, Widow	44	1	2 0	Family	*Back Lanes.*
Chase's Child	—	—	2 6	Deserted by Father ..	*Seething Well.*
Chambers, Rich. and Wife	60	4	5 0	Illness and family	*Back Lanes.*
Chapman, Widow	71	—	3 0	Infirm	*London Road.*
Chester, Widow	70	—	3 0	Infirm	*Hogg's Mill.*
Chennell's Child	5	—	2 6	Illegitimate	*Fair Field.*
Churchill, Charles, & Wife	40	5	5 0	Family	*London Street.*
Clark, Widow	59	—	2 0	Infirm	*Back Lanes.*
Clark, Widow	36	1	2 0	Family	*London Road.*
Clark, Widow	77	—	3 0	Illness	*Dulwich.*
Dandy, Widow	57	1	2 6	Family	*Church Yard Row.*
Dalton, Mary	73	—	2 6	——	*Oxted, Surrey.*
Earl, Ruth	61	—	2 0	Infirm	*Towns End.*
Farmer, Daniel	73	—	2 0	Illness	*Lion and Lamb Yard.*
Farmer, Thomas, and Wife	65	—	5 0	The Man blind	*Tolworth.*
Farmer, Widow	87	—	3 0	Infirm	*Hogg's Mill.*
Fairey, Elizabeth	53	—	2 0	Infirm	*Barking.*
Figgett, Margaret	47	2	4 0	Family	*Gillingham, Kent.*
** Fowler, William, & Wife	42	6	4 0	Family	*Heathen Street.*
Foster's, Captain, Child ...	7	—	2 6	Illegitimate	*Kent Road.*
Fry, Elizabeth	73	—	1 6	Infirm	*Sussex.*
** Fray, Widow	35	3	6 0	Family	*Back Lanes.*
Fricker's Child	13	—	3 0	Father dead	*Isleworth.*
Fruin's Child	8	—	2 6	Father dead	*Shepherds Bush.*
Frost, Charlotte	23	—	3 0	Fits	*Wimbledon.*
Gardner, George	67	—	2 6	Infirm	*Surbiton.*
** Gally, William, and Wife	49	6	6 0	Family	*Fair Field.*
Gray, Widow	76	—	2 6	Infirm	*Wanderings.*
Gray's Children	—	4	7 0	Family	*Hampton Wick.*
Grey, Martha	6	—	4 6	Illegitimate	*Walthamstow Workhouse.*
Hamilton, Widow	50	—	3 0	Illness	*Back Lanes.*
Harrad, Ann	65	—	2 6	Illness	*Towns End.*
Harrison's Children	—	2	2 0	Family	*Apple Market.*
Harrison's, Harriott, Child	1	—	2 6	Illegitimate	*Fair Field.*
Hackman's, Mary, Child ..	3	—	2 6	Illegitimate	*Hampton Wick.*
Herrick, Widow	80	—	2 0	Infirm	*Hogg's Mill.*
Heater's, Mary, Child	4	—	2 0	Illegitimate	*Cobham.*
Hill, Benjamin, and Wife	33	5	5 0	Family and Wife ill ..	*Wanderings.*
Holles, Widow	68	—	3 0	Illness	*Horse Fair.*
* Honey, Widow	51	2	5 0	Family	*Horse Fair.*
Jane and Wife	52	2	5 0	Illness and family	*London.*
Jacob's Child	5	—	2 6	Illegitimate	*Clandon, Surrey.*
Jeffries's Children	—	5	7 0	Father dead	*Market Place.*
Jeffries, Widow	65	—	1 6	Infirm	*Surbiton.*
Jeffries's Child	14	—	2 6	Fits	*Surbiton.*
Jefkins, Widow	74	—	2 6	Infirm	*Wanderings.*
Johnston, Thomas, and Wife	81	—	5 0	Infirm	*Apple Market.*

NAMES OF PAUPERS.	Age.	Number of Children Dependent.	Amount of Relief. s. d.	CAUSE OF RELIEF.	OBSERVATIONS.
Keen, Widow	65	—	2 0	Infirm	*Weston's Park.*
Kemp, Robert, and Wife ..	39	3	3 0	Family	*Hampton Wick.*
Knott, Elizabeth	57	—	2 6	Infirm	*London Road.*
Lalham and Wife	60	3	7 0	Illness	*Back Lanes.*
Lawrence, Widow	47	2	5 0	Family	*Surbiton.*
Lilburn's Child	16	—	1 0	Fits	*Bridge Street.*
Line's, Jane, Children	—	3	6 0	Family	*Church Yard Row.*
Long, Widow	57	4	5 0	Family	*Wanderings.*
Marshall's Children	—	3	3 0	Family	*Norbiton Common.*
Martin, William	71	—	1 0	Infirm	*Brentford.*
Merrit, Widow	62	—	2 0	Infirm	*Rockwell's Rents.*
Melsom, Widow	69	—	2 0	Infirm	*Back Lanes.*
Miller's Child	9	—	2 6	Deserted by Father ..	*Hampton Court.*
Milliss, Samuel, and Wife	45	2	5 0	Illness	*Church Yard Row.*
Mitchell's Child	—	—	3 6	Orphan	*Chobham.*
Nash, Ann	90	—	2 0	Infirm	*Richmond.*
New, Widow	73	—	2 0	Infirm	*Apple Market.*
Neville's, Mary, Child	—	—	3 0	Illegitimate	*Back Lanes.*
Nichols, Thomas	37	—	5 0	Fits	*Thames Street.*
Page's Child	—	—	4 0	Very ill—since dead ..	*Wandsworth.*
Paine, Widow	58	1	3 0	Family	*Norbiton Common.*
Paine, Elizabeth	64	1	1 6	Family	*Surbiton.*
Parker, Henry	77	—	2 6	Infirm	*Rockwell's Rents.*
Parker, Widow	56	—	1 6	Infirm	*Brewhouse Yard.*
Parker's Children	—	5	20 0	Orphans	*Godalming.*
Peters, Edward, and Wife	52	4	5 0	Family and illness	*Church Yard Row.*
** Pearman, Rob. and Wife	45	7	1 0	Family	*London Road.*
Pewsey, Widow	29	2	5 0	Family	*Heathen Street.*
** Peacock, Widow	36	4	10 0	Illness and family	*London Street.*
Pierson, Ann	53	—	2 0	Infirm	*Back Lanes.*
Pierson, Sarah	45	—	2 0	Infirm	*Back Lanes.*
Piper, Widow	62	—	2 6	Infirm	*Horse Fair.*
Pricket, Widow	61	—	2 6	Infirm	*Marsh.*
Rowe, Widow	71	—	2 6	Infirm	*Heathen Street.*
Robertson, Eleanor	4	—	2 0	Deserted by Father ..	*London Road.*
Russell, Mary	84	—	3 0	Infirm	*Isleworth.*
Salter, Charles	70	—	5 0	Infirm	*Clattern Bridge.*
Sanders, Widow	65	—	2 0	Infirm	*Fulham.*
* Shotter, William, & Wife	32	3	1 0	Family	*London Street.*
** Smith, Widow	41	6	12 0	Family, & 1 child afflicted	*Surbiton.*
Smith, Oakley, and Wife ..	38	7	3 0	Family	*Heathen Street.*
Smith, William, and Wife	40	5	3 0	Family	*Back Lanes.*
Smith, Widow	70	—	2 6	Infirm	*Back Lanes.*
Smith, Widow	61	—	2 0	Illness	*Horse Fair.*
Spencer's Child	2	—	2 6	Father at Sea	*London Street.*
Spong's Children	—	5	12 0	Family	*Malden.*
Steers, Thomas, and Wife	40	4	5 0	Ill and out of work	*Wandsworth.*
Stacey, Henry, and Wife	60	5	2 6	Family	*Horse Fair.*
Strudwick's Children	—	4	10 0	Family	*Fulham.*
Steptoe's Children	—	2	4 0	Illegitimate	*Apple Market.*
Steptoe's, Widow	73	—	4 0	Very infirm	*Apple Market.*
Sykes, Joanna	—	—	2 6	For a Child	*St. Andrews, Herts.*
Taylor, Widow	84	—	4 0	Very infirm	*Towns End.*
Taylor, Henry, and Wife ..	32	3	3 0	Illness	*Surbiton Common.*
** Taylor, Joseph, and Wife	36	7	4 0	Family	*Surbiton Common.*
Todman, Richard	72	—	3 0	Infirm	*Chertsey.*
Turrell, Widow	78	—	2 0	Infirm	*Sunbury.*
Turner, Widow	65	—	2 6	Infirm	*Church Yard Row.*
Turner, Thomas, and Wife	41	2	4 0	Wife and Daughter ill	*Hampton Wick.*
Vaughan, George, and Wife	34	4	5 0	Family	*Brentford.*
Vaughan, John, and Wife	69	—	2 6	Infirm	*Coodham, Kent.*
Vickery, Widow	67	—	2 6	Infirm	*Wood Street.*
Vinnacombe	70	—	2 0	Infirm	*Weston Green.*
Waight, Widow	39	3	6 0	Family	*Hampton Wick.*
Walters, Widow	75	—	2 0	Infirm	*London Road.*
Walker's, Mary, Child ...	3	—	2 0	Illegitimate	*London.*
*** Warren, Tho. and Wife	69	3	5 0	Illness and Family	*Ham.*
Warwick, Ann	32	3	6 0	Deserted by Husband	*Surbiton.*
Waters, Widow	72	—	2 6	Infirm	*Heathen Street.*
West's Child	7	—	2 0	Illegitimate	*Wanderings.*
West, Henry, and Wife ..	43	5	5 0	Family	*Norbiton Common.*
* West, Widow	45	2	3 0	Family	*Bridge Street.*
West, Sarah	60	—	1 6	——	*Merton.*
Wells, Mary	41	—	2 6	Infirm	*Wandsworth.*
Welling, Widow	67	—	2 0	Infirm	*Back Lanes.*
Westbrook, Widow	62	—	2 0	Infirm	*Wanderings.*
White, George, and Wife	43	2	2 0	Now discontinued	*Horse Fair.*
Williams, Watkins, & Wife	43	3	8 0	Very ill	*London.*
Wood, Widow	65	—	2 0	Infirm	*Bridge Street.*
Wood, James, and Wife ..	57	5	5 0	Family	*Heathen Street.*
Woodman's Child	6	—	2 0	Illegitimate	*Effingham.*
Wright, Roger	82	—	2 6	Infirm	*Horse Fair.*

OCCASIONAL RELIEF.

NAMES OF PAUPERS.	Age.	Number of Children Dependent.	Amount of Relief.	CAUSE OF RELIEF.	OBSERVATIONS.
Bullbeck, Wm. and Wife ..	—	2	Variable	Out of work	*Wanderings.*
Coster, James, and Wife ..	—	5	—	Out of work	*Whitton.*
Curry, John, and Wife ..	—	4	—	Neglect of Family	*Kingston Workhouse.*
Egerton and Wife	—	3	—	Wife's illness	*Cobham.*
Foy, John, and Wife	—	1	—	Illness and out of work	*Towns End.*
Fry, George, and Wife ...	—	1	—	Out of work	*Hampton Wick.*
Gray and Wife	—	1	—	Out of work	*Hampton Wick.*
Gray, James, and Wife ...	—	3	—	Ditto and children ill ..	*Wanderings.*
Hardwick and Wife	—	3	—	Illness	*London Street.*
Holly, Stephen, and Wife	—	3	—	Out of work and illness	*London Street.*
Holland, Rich. and Wife ..	—	2	—	Illness	*Back Lanes.*
Hunt, William	—		Variable	Out of work	*Church Yard Row.*
Jeffries, Joseph, and Wife	—	2	—	Out of work	*Surbiton.*
Lee, James	17		—	Illness	*Wanderings.*
Morris	—		—	Out of work	*Wandsworth.*
Neemes, Robert	—		—	Out of work	*Back Lanes.*
Pavey, William, and Wife	—	1	—	Out of work and illness	*Thames Street.*
Palmer, Ezra, and Wife ..	—	2	—	Very ill	*Horse Fair.*
Smith, David	—		—	Out of work	*Surbiton.*
Turrell, Elizabeth	—	1	—	Out of work	*Back Lanes.*
Wild, William	—		—	Out of work	*Seething Well.*
Windebanks, Wm. and Wife	—		—	Out of work	*Hampton Wick.*

The *** attached to the Names denote the number of Quartern Loaves received Weekly by those Persons, in addition to the Money.

The Overseers, wishing as far as possible, to guard the Funds entrusted to their Management, from Imposition, have published the foregoing List of Persons, with their Residences, and Amount of Relief now afforded; and should any of the Parishioners be aware of any just ground for diminishing or discontinuing the present Allowance, they are requested to inform the Overseers. The Overseers solicit the attention of Gentlemen to the employing of Parishioners, as many applications for Relief, arise out of the want of regular Employment.

EDWARD KENT,
J. S. HAYCRAFT,
S. ALLENBY,
JOHN REED, } OVERSEERS.

KINGSTON, June 21, 1820.

J. ATTFIELD, Printer, Market Place, Kingston.

A published list of paupers in Kingston, 1820.

Parliamentary Papers

Parliamentary papers are also a useful and under-used source. A general introduction can be found in an online research guide *Printed Parliamentary Papers* at **www.nationalarchives.gov.uk/catalogue**.

The National Archives has a set of these Papers. They are now available online in the reading rooms at Kew, in a fully searchable form.

Parliamentary Papers are well indexed. The best index is at **www. bopcris. ac.uk,** although it is not complete.

There are several types of record that may be of use:

Reports and papers of Royal Commissions and other enquiries

There were numerous Royal Commissions and other enquiries into the condition of the poor. The most important of these were the Royal Commissions of 1832-1834 and 1905-1908. As well as detailed reports both commissions ordered that accompanying evidence be published.

As part of the evidence presented to the Commission of 1832, overseers or poor law officials were asked to complete a questionnaire about the provision made for poor relief in their parish, but only a fifth of parishes bothered to reply. Disappointed by the poor response, the commissioners decided to send a number of assistant commissioners round the country in 1832 and 1833 to report on the position locally. Another fifth of parishes were visited in total. Although sketchy this evidence offers a unique view of the lives of poor people in the early 1830s.

There were also a number of parliamentary committees which looked at aspects of the poor law or indeed the condition of the poor in general. The evidence presented can be a vivid insight into the life of the pauper. The best known of these enquiries examined conditions in Andover workhouse in 1847.

Annual reports of the Poor Law Commissioners and their successors

The Poor Law Commissioners, and their successors, presented an annual report to Parliament summarising their work during the previous year. Particularly in the early years these reports offer another illuminating insight into how the Poor Law operated.

Individual returns and circulars

These papers also contain individual returns made to Parliament, normally at the request of an MP. Often they are just for a single year or just for a few years. Among this material are the returns of officials employed at Lady Day [March 25th], 1848, listing people by union, with details of salary, age and period of service with their present employers, and lists for a number of years during the 1860s of paupers who had been in the workhouse for more than five years.

Alternatives to the Poor Law

There were usually alternative options to the Poor Law. Indeed because it was so hated, it was often seen as the last resort. Particularly after 1834, the poor law authorities were generally only willing to assist the most destitute, the most helpless and those with the greatest long term needs. For everybody else there was a range of alternatives which could be used depending on circumstance and inclination.

At a very basic level friends, neighbours and work colleagues would have a whip round to help a family in temporary trouble. Many observers, agreed with Friedrich Engels who said in the 1840s that "although workers cannot afford to give to charity on the same scale as the middle class they are nevertheless more charitable in every way." And sixty years later the Reverend William Conybeare claimed that it was "largely the kindness of poor to poor which stands between our current civilisation and revolution."

"I'm proud of the poor," the East End trade unionist and poor law guardian Will Crook wrote, "And I declare it's a dirty insult for outsiders to say that these people are degraded by the feeble efforts I make as a guardian to give bread to the hungry. It's nothing to what they do for each other. That woman sharing her bread is typical of what you'll find in every street and corner of Poplar, where the pinch of hunger is felt."

Short-term loans could be arranged from pawnbrokers, by pawning a handkerchief or an overcoat. It was a staple of many working class budgets. Alison Backhouse's study of the pledgebook of George Fette, a York pawnbroker in the 1770s, suggests that many of his customers were regulars pledging small items of bedding or clothing twice a week.

Shops might be persuaded to offer goods on account for regular customers in temporary difficulties. It was one service which street corner shops offered that the high street stores would not, although there was always the risk to the shopkeeper that a customer would default. In Salford [Lancashire], Robert Roberts' mother ran one such shop before the First World War and sometimes grumbled that she was in effect a banker to the community.

Pawnbrokers' Records

A few pawnbrokers' pledge books survive at local record offices. One for York was analysed by Alison Backhouse in *The Worm-Eaten Waistcoat* (Backhouse, 2007) with some details, see - **www.webworms.talktalk.net**. Memoirs of growing up in poverty can give a flavour of how families supported each other in times of crisis.

Pensions

Until 1908 there was no such thing as universal pensions for the elderly who were expected to work until they were unable to any longer. The lucky were then cared for by their families (possibly helped by out-relief provided by the parish or poor law guardians) or admitted to an almshouse; the unlucky entered the workhouse.

One of the few attractions of service in the Army and Navy was the grant of a pension for honourable service after discharge. In a number of workhouses there were sizeable numbers of service pensioners who were paid their pensions quarterly. Workhouses tended to empty out for a few days or weeks after payday while the money was frittered away. Railway Companies and the Post Office also paid pensions, but most other companies or institutions did not.

From the 1880s there were various campaigns for an old age pension, but it was not until 1908 that it was introduced. Each man or woman over 70 now received five shillings a week of right, provided they had an income of less than ten shillings a week. Pensions were collected from post offices in order to remove any stigma of the poor law. However applicants were ineligible if they had been paupers or had had a criminal record. In practice, however, this was widely ignored by the local committees that administered the new system. The Pension was hardly generous, but it gave the poor some financial independence. Thankfully for family historians the 1841 and 1851 censuses were used to prove eligibility for individuals for a pension and were not destroyed as they might otherwise have been.

Pension Records

Pension Records for the Army, Navy and railway companies are at The National Archives at Kew. None are yet online, although the soldiers' documents in series WO 97, prove that a pension was awarded, can be found on Findmypast. There are various research guides to help you find your way around these records. The British Postal Museum and Archive has various series of records for postmen who received pensions. Details at **http://catalogue.postalheritage.org.uk**.

No records of individual old age pensions survive although you may find appeals in the papers of local pension committees, which have been deposited at county record offices. Before 1908 you may find material in the paperwork relating to out-relief kept by the relieving officers who were employed by the poor law guardians in their case books and before them the accounts of the overseers of the poor.

Friendly Societies

From the late eighteenth century and well into the twentieth century most working class men were members of a friendly society, where for a few pence a week they would receive benefits in times of unemployment or sickness. At the height of the movement, in 1901, just over half the adult male population of England and Wales were members of such societies like the Ancient Order of Foresters, the Oddfellows or the temperance Rechabites. Even a century earlier a third and probably more, were members. Membership was not just the privilege of the more prosperous working class, most societies had unskilled or poorly paid members.

Social activity was another reason for joining. Many societies engaged in some form of harmless ritual based on Masonic rites, which gave members a feeling of belonging. The big event of the year was often a parade to the parish church for a service before sitting down to a large dinner.

Towards the end of the nineteenth century, societies typically charged weekly premiums of between fourpence and sixpence for basic sickness and burial benefits. These were amounts that a working man in regular employment earning between 16 and 20 shillings a week could afford. But even these premiums might be beyond the reach of those without jobs or who were only employed sporadically. In particular those who could not hold down a steady job, or lost such a position, found it difficult to maintain regular payments, so would lose any benefits they might have accrued from membership.

Records of Friendly Societies

Because there were so many friendly societies it may be impossible to work out which one your ancestor belonged to. Occasionally you may have photographs of regalia (often referred to as jewels), which look Masonic but is more likely to be that of a friendly society. The Library and Museum of Freemasonry at Freemasons Hall, 60 Great Queen Street, London WC2B 5AZ, **www.free masonry.london.museum** may be able to help identify regalia.

Societies were either independent, or affiliated to larger organisations. Many independent societies date from the eighteenth century, and often catered for a particular group of workers. They were controlled to a degree by local clergymen and other bigwigs. Affiliated societies took off in the 1820s, and were popular because they had financial security as the result of being part of a larger organisation. The Ancient Order of Foresters was the largest of these affiliated bodies.

Only about 5 per cent of records of friendly societies have been deposited in local record offices, generally for branches of national friendly societies, rather than for independent local societies. Only rarely do you can find any records of individual members although there may be mentions in minute books, annual reports and the like if your forebear became an active member.

Several of the larger friendly societies maintain their own archives. These include:

Ancient Order of Foresters Heritage Trust, Foresters House, 29-33 Shirley Road,College Place, Southampton SO15 2FE, **www.aoforestersheritage. com/Archive.html**

The Oddfellows have put some of their archives online at **www. oddfellows.co. uk/Site/Content/Archives.aspx**

The best introduction is Roger Logan, *Friendly Society Records* (Federation of Family History Societies, 2000). See also Dan Weinbren, 'Mutually Beneficial: records of friendly societies' *Ancestors magazine* (June 2004).

The Friendly Society Research Group may also be able to help and has some interesting pages at **www.open.ac.uk/socialsciences/friendly-societies-research-group.**

Charities and almshouses

Another alternative was to seek help from a charity. To the Victorians many social ills could be cured by a healthy dose of philanthropy. As a result most towns and villages had a wide range of charities which gave grants and pensions to the poor, ranging from almshouses to bread and coals to poor widows and small payments to the temporarily destitute and their families. The 1906 Royal Commission on the Poor Law wrote that: "No one can have taken part in an enquiry such as ours without being impressed... by the multitude and variety of voluntary organisations established for ameliorating the condition of the poor, the large sums which pass through their hands and the amount of time and effort devoted to them by a veritable army of charitable workers."

In Lambeth, for example, Jeffrey Cox found 'at least 57 mothers' meetings, 36 Temperance societies for children, 25 savings banks or penny banks, 24 Christian Endeavour societies, 21 boot, coal, blanket, or clothing clubs, and two maternity societies. There were 16 nurses and two part time doctors as well as a part time dentist in addition to those sponsored by the provident dispensaries which were closely linked to the churches. Furthermore there were two 'servants' registries, two lodging registries, two 'industrial societies' which employed women at needlework, one burial guild, one convalescent home, one hostel for the dying, one invalid kitchen, cripples' classes, a children's playtime, a day nursery, a 'prostitutes institute', several libraries, and dozens of Sunday schools in addition to the extensive work of extra-parochial and trans-denominational organisations.' In addition almost half of the Nonconformist chapels and all the Anglican parishes in the borough also provided relief to the poor in cash or kind.

The provision of charity, particularly those which attempted to help the very poor, was haphazard. They were mostly concentrated in the older cathedral cities and market towns, with fewer in the newer industrial towns of the Midlands and the North. In rural areas there were far fewer charities. Here it was the Anglican parish priest who was generally the first person to turn to.

Charities were also particular about who they supported. They were there to help, in the phrase of the period the 'deserving poor' that is those who were industrious but had fallen on hard times through no fault of their own, for whom a small grant, loan or donation of bread or coal would help the applicant become self-sufficient again, not the 'undeserving' who deserved nothing but the workhouse.

William Grisewood, secretary of the Liverpool's Central Relief Society, spoke for many when he, argued that it: "… used to be said the persons aided by the Society belonged to a stratum just above the pauper class, and this is still in measure true, our aim being to prevent, when possible the indigent from sinking into that class."

In general, charities wanted to help people who would benefit quickly (and gratefully) from support rather than cases which might be a drain on resources for many years. As C S Loch, secretary of the Charity Organisation Society, once put it, the question was "not whether a person was 'deserving' or 'undeserving', but whether grant the facts the distress can be stayed and self-support sustained."

It is clear that charities often helped people who fitted their own perception of the 'deserving poor', such as aged men and women who had been regular church goers all their lives or orphaned children of soldiers and sailors killed on active service. Undoubtedly the system was easy to abuse by the poor, who took advantage of the duplication between rival charities and the gullibility of potential donors.

It was to prevent abuses like these that led to the establishment of Charity Organisation Society (COS) in 1869. The COS sought to bring scientific method to charities through the thorough investigation of those seeking aid and to co-ordinate the work of other charities. In particular it encouraged local charities to rigorously interview applicants before offering assistance and to co-operate in establishing registers of the local poor, ideally in conjunction with the local poor law authorities, to ensure that people were not claiming more than they were due. The methods and arguments of the COS also had an impact on many poor law guardians in the late nineteenth century.

The COS soon acquired a reputation for meanness. Its critics, of whom there were many, claimed that its abbreviation stood for 'Cringe or Starve'.

There were earlier forms of charity generally founded by a particular benefactor, such as a local merchant or landowner. The benefaction might take the form of an almshouse, a school, scholarships for apprentices, or the annual provision of bread or coals to the deserving elderly, sometimes known as dole funds. My school (Newport Grammar in Essex) was founded for poor boys by Dame Joyce Frankland in memory of her son who died after falling off his horse in the village in 1588.

The oldest charities are medieval in origin, such as the Hospital of St Cross in Winchester which was founded in 1129 and still looks after elderly men and offers bread and beer to travellers as its founder Bishop Blois intended. In County Durham, Christ's Hospital was established in 1181 by King Stephen's nephew Hugh de Puiset, Bishop of Durham. It continued as a lazar-house until 1434 when it became an almshouse for the poor brethren of the parish of Thornley, although it did retain space for two lepers "if they can be found." Today it provides sheltered housing and respite care for the elderly. The provision of almshouses, dole funds and so on is very patchy. Richmond in Surrey has eight almshouses, for example, while its neighbour Kingston has just one, although Kingston had at least one school while there was none in Richmond. Almshouses are likely to be found in towns which were well established by the medieval and Tudor times.

ORDERS and RESOLVES, made the fifth day of November, ANNO DOMINI 1669, and in the one and twentieth year of the Reign, of our Sovereign Lord Charles the Second, &c. By the Governors of the Almshouses, in Kingston-upon-Thames, newly erected, given by WILLIAM CLEEVE, ESQUIRE, deceased, for the better ·ordering and managing of the Almshouses, and the Revenues thereto belonging, according to the pious Intent of the said WILLIAM CLEEVE.

FIRSTLY.   THAT the six rooms of the said Almshouses on the West side the Hall there, shall be for six poor aged and single Men, the other six rooms on the eastside of the said Hall, for six poor aged and single Women, to be chosen by the said Governors for the time being, or the major part of them, at their public meeting in the Guildhall of the said Town.

SECONDLY.   THAT no swearer, drunkard, or debauched person, shall be admitted into any of the said Almshouses, nor any having a dangerous infections disease, Lunatic person, or common beggar.

THIRDLY.   THAT all the said Almsmen and Women, shall duly every Sunday at the times for public worship, morning and afternoon, repair to the parish Church of Kingston, and there remain orderly and soberly, during the time of public prayers and preaching, unless they shall be hindered by sickness, or by some other cause, which the said ·,Governors shall allow of for excuse, on pain to forfeit for every such default twelve-pence, and for a wilful neglect by the space of a month without such cause as aforesaid, to be fined or expelled the said Almshouse, at the discretion of the Governors.

FOURTHLY.   THAT all the poor Men and Women, during their respective abodes, in the said Almshouses, shall demean themselves honestly, and soberly, spending their time in praying, reading, hearing the word, or other religious duties, or in some honest employment, acording to their ability, and shall endeavour to relieve and be helpful one to another, and in case of sickness, those that are in health, shall by turns, attend and watch with them that are sick, the Men only with the Men, the Women with the Men, or Women, as need shall require, or they be able, on pain that every neglect they be severally fined, as the Governors shall think fit.

FIFTHLY.   THAT none of the poor Men, or Women, shall swear, curse, revile, rail, strike, hurt, be contentious, carry tales, make debate amongst their fellows, or offer just cause of offence to any other, nor shall they take inmates to lodge, nor frequent any alehouse, tippling house, or suspected place, nor lodge any night out of his or her house, without leave from the Treasurer, neither shall any of them use any unlawful game, noisome or offensive trade, work, or dealing, keep any poultry, or other thing offensive to the rest, nor shall keep any of their Houses nasty or foul, receive any stolen goods, or countenance any that do the same, upon pain to forfeit, for either of the same offences, twelve-pence, and if then shall after two or three warnings, again offend, to be expelled the House for ever.

SIXTHLY.   THAT all the forfeitures and fines, which shall be incurred by any of the said poor people, for any offence, shall be deducted or abated out of the pension of such person offending, by the Treasurer, to be disposed of, as the Governors shall order and direct.

SEVENTHLY.

Rules and Regulations for people living in Cleeves Almshouses, 1669. The merchant William Cleeve in his will of 1665, left money "for the erecting of a building of a convenient house for six poor men and six poor women of honest life and reputation". The almshouses in

2

SEVENTHLY. THAT no person shall dwell in either of the said Houses, or enjoy the pensions assigned and appointed to each of them, longer than he or she, shall orderly and well behave themselves, yielding obedience to these, and all other orders of the Governors, or hereafter to be made, and if any of them, upon examination of the Governors, shall be thought fit to be expelled and discharged, and shall not submit ot the Governors orders therein, then his or her pension to cease, and if after two months warning, they shall not depart, then his or her goods to be put forth, and another placed therein.

EIGHTHLY. THAT the Governors for the time being, shall upon the fifth day of November, yearly, meet together at the Guildhall of the said Town, unless the same day happen to be upon Saturday, or Sunday, and if so then upon the Monday following such fifth day of November, and then and there choose, among themselves, a Treasurer to receive all monies, rents, and profits, of and belonging to the said Almshouses, and pay unto the said poor Men and Women, the pensions allowed to them, and then and there, shall give up his account, as Treasurer for the year past, of the revenue of the said Almshouses, for the monies by him received, and disbursed, according to the trust of the said Governors, and cause the same to be entered into a book, and fairly written, and such account, to be subscribed by the Governors then present, and cause the monies there remaining, to be paid over to the succeeding Treasurer, in their presence, and a memorial thereof to be entered in the said book, and the succeeding Treasurer, to subscribe his name, as an acknowledgement of the receipt of the Money so accounted to remain, and mentioned to be paid over to such succeeding Treasurer.

NINTHLY. THAT the Gown, and Badge thereupon, of every poor Man and Woman, dying, and also all the sea-coals, wood, and other fewel, allowed and provided by the said Governors, or Treasurer, and which shall be left, and remaining in the House, at the time of him or her dying, shall not go to any stranger, or kindred, of the deceased party, but shall be wholly left, to be at the disposing of the said Governors, for the time being, or the major part of them.

TENTHLY. THAT if any of the Governors, shall make default to meet in the Guildhall of the said Town, upon the fifth day of November, yearly, unless the same day happen upon the Saturday, or the Sunday, and if so it happen upon either of those days, then upon the Monday following, for the electing of a treasurer, as aforesaid, then every such Governor, making default upon the same day, shall forfeit Two Shillings and Sixpence, to go and be for the use of the said poor Men and Women, except he or they do shew snch sufficient cause, as shall satisfy the said Governors, or the major part of them.

ELEVENTHLY. THAT if the person that shall be hereafter chosen to be Treasurer, shall refuse to be Treasurer, that then the Treasurer elected, and refusing as aforesaid, shall forfeit five pounds, to go and be to the use of the poor people of the said Almshouses, as the Governors, or the major part of them shall think fit,

TWELFTHLY. THAT these orders shall be read to the poor people, once every year, yearly, by the Treasurer, in the presence of the Governors, in the Hall of the said Almshouses.

THIRTEENTHLY. THAT if any lands, tenements, goods, or chattles, do at any time hereafter descend or come, to any of the poor Men, or Women, already placed in, or hereafter to be placed in the said Almshouse, sufficient for the maintenance of such poor person respectively, or in case any of the said poor persons Men or Women, depart this life, that then the Treasurer for the time being, shall within two days, after the descent, or coming of such Estate, or other goods, to such person or persons, or of the respective death of any such poor Man, or Woman, give Notice to the Governors, that so a Meeting of the said Governors be appointed within ten days after such last mentioned notice, for the election of a person to succeed in the said Almshouse, in the room of the person so deceased,

LASTLY

Kingston were built in 1669, extended in 1889 and remodelled in 1994 and still perform a useful service. (Royal Borough of Kingston-upon-Thames, document reference KG 24/1/2)

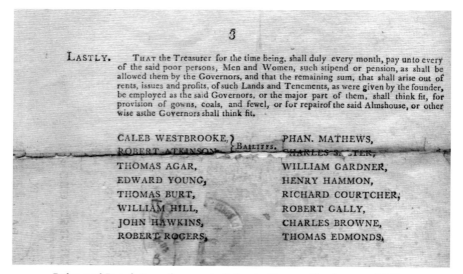

Rules and Regulations for people living in Cleeves Almshouses, 1669.

Records of Charities

Surviving records of charities are likely to be found at local record offices, although records for most small charities have long been lost. They are listed on the National Register of Archives (**www.nationalarchives.gov.uk/ nra**). The Hospital Records Database provides details of the location of hospitals many of which began as charitable or voluntary foundations (**www.nationalarchives.gov.uk/hospitalrecords**)

Charities which are still in existence tend to keep their own archives, which they may be willing to let you consult (sometimes for a small fee). The largest such archive is probably maintained by Barnado's, which has detailed records about all the boys and girls it has helped since the 1870s. Details at **www.barnardos.org.uk/who_we_are/history/family_history_service.htm**. A fascinating history of some of the children cared for by the National Children's Homes is at **www.theirhistory.co.uk**. In Scotland there was Quarriers see **www.quarriers.org.uk**.

You may find case reports on individuals (often closed for 75 years or longer), board and committee minute books which may include discussions about individual applications. Also useful are annual reports which tend to be a summary of the year's work and an appeal for funds. The reports may describe some of the cases helped, but the recipients may only be identified by initials. Reports for schools, however, may well list prize winners and indicate where students went after they left.

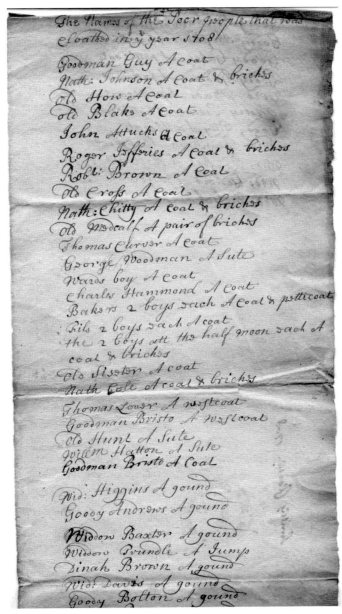

List of poor people's clothes by the Henry Smith Charity in Kingston, 1708. (Royal Borough of Kingston-on-Thames, document reference KG 14/2/1

Religious charities

As might be expected Christian churches and Jewish synagogues were very active in helping co-religionists as well, and in some cases, using charity to try to make converts. In this they were following teachings in the Bible which exhorted readers to help the poor for their lay salvation: "But rather give alms of such things as ye have; and, behold, all things are clean unto you" (Luke 11:41).

Church charities were particularly important in places where there had been mass immigration and little sense of natural community. In Catholic parishes, for example, much effort was centred around local St Vincent de Paul societies which helped poor parishioners, as well as ensuring that they were not tempted by the secular society in which they lived.

In the East End there were numerous charities to help Jews newly arrived from Eastern Europe. The Soup Kitchen in Brune Street, for example, was built in 1902 to provide charitable support for Jewish immigrants. As late as the 1950s it was still regularly feeding 1500 people. But the building itself asserted that the Jewish community could provide for its own. And the ornate façade testifies to the wealth of the Jewish community, offering inspiration to less fortunate co-religionists that with hard work and determination that they too could prosper.

In both rural and urban areas Anglican clergymen were directly involved helping their poor parishioners. Randall Davidson, Archbishop of Canterbury, told the Royal Commission on the Poor Law in 1909 that "there are not a class of educated men throughout England who necessarily know so much about the daily life of the poor as do the clergy both in urban and rural parishes." This was especially true in the countryside. The Royal Commission found that in villages: "The clergyman, indeed, seems to be almost as natural a person to turn to for assistance as the relieving officer himself." This is perhaps not surprising considering the hostility the poor law and its servants evoked among the poor.

This was not only a function of Anglican clergy. In other denominations, particular the Catholic, priests were (and remain) unpaid social workers. In his autobiography, Pat O'Mara, describes his experience as a tubercular child in Liverpool in the 1930s: "The following day with the frenzy so characteristic of her when danger threatened her children, my mother bought Father Wilson from St Peter's to see me. He took one look at me and the room and my mother and immediately got in touch with Miss Margaret Bevan." She was a famous local charity worker who arranged for him to be sent to a sanatorium in West Kirby (on the Wirral).

There were a myriad of charitable bodies. The Anglicans had a vast number from the Girls Friendly Society, which helped girls and young women, to bread and coal, and clothing and shoe clubs where people could put by a few pence each month with the rest made up from donations from richer parishioners. Such clubs could be very popular. Ten per cent of the population of Richmond were members of the clothing club in the 1860s. Other denominations maintained similar charities for their members.

The Records of Church Charities

As with all charity records the survival of material relating to church or religious charities is patchy. The best place to start is the local record office or local studies library, where you may find annual reports and possibly case books recording how co-religionists were helped. For example, the East Yorkshire Record Office has the Beverley Wesleyan Circuit Account Book recording money given to poor members between 1868 and 1929, generally just a shilling or two but no doubt very much welcome at the time. Occasionally case books or minute books survive which discuss individuals. Tower Hamlets Local Studies Library has the minute books of St George's Lutheran Church Society of Ladies Charity (1821-1846, 1868-1883) which record the cases of the poor members of their congregation many of which were immigrants from Germany. On 10 December 1868, the book notes:

"SILBERBACH, Alexander and Charlotte, 54 Richard Street, last relieved 6th December 1866. Still residing at 54[formerly 9] Richard Street, circumstances quite unaltered, husband still in Colney Hatch Asylum. 2 boys of 9 and 7, both in Infants School, 1 girl of 14, free of our school. Full suit, 2 pairs of shoes, 1 shawl and 2 tailors suits [ordered]."

N.B. Alexander was a former sugar baker who died in Colney Hatch Asylum in 1907 but can be identified in the 1881 and 1891 Censuses by his initials, age, occupation and place of birth Koenigsburg, Prussia which corresponds to his entry in the 1861 Census. His case papers including a photograph can now be seen in the records for Colney Hatch in London Metropolitan Archives having earlier been subject to a 100 year closure rule.

You may well find reports from charities and accounts of their activities (particularly fundraising) in parish magazines and their equivalents which most Anglican parishes and many non-conformist chapels, Catholic parishes and Jewish communities were publishing from the 1860s. In January 1893, for example, the Appleby Magna parish magazine in Leicestershire reported on a concert held to benefit Barnardo's Homes: "The programme was long and of varied character consisting of solos, choruses, and dialogues for the most part by children of the National Schools. It was opened by a prologue well and distinctly spoken by Charles Garrod, after which the children sang the "Legend of the Bells" from Les Cloches de Corneville in excellent time and tune..." The survival of this surprisingly neglected source for family historians (they usually include details of those recently baptised, married and buried) is patchy, but again the local record office or local studies library is the best place to look. Extracts from a few parish magazines can be found online.

Local newspapers may also contain reports of charity meetings and fundraising events with names of officers, speakers and singers. In Shropshire *The Wellington Journal* for 5 May 1900 reported a meeting of the Pleasant Sunday Afternoon Movement (PSA) a nonconformist organisation in the town: "The address at this class on Sunday was given by Mr James Clay, and there was a good attendance. A solo by Mr G.F. Blakeley was well rendered. The president, Mr George Wilkinson, occupied the chair."

There were also national charities which had backing from a particular denomination. Often this is clear in the title, but occasionally it is not. The National Children's Home was a Wesleyan Methodist Charity, while the Poor Waifs and Strays (later the Children's Society) was Anglican. Where records survive they are likely to be held at a national repository. The National Register of Archives should be able to help. Records of individual cases may no longer survive or access may be restricted for 75 or 100 years.

Over the past 145 years the Salvation Army has helped many of the poorest in society, although the excessive religious moralising probably put off many whom they were trying to help. Tramps and the homeless often avoided Salvation Army shelters for this reason. The Salvation Army International Heritage Centre has full records of the Army's activities but very little about the people it helped. You can contact them at House 14, The William Booth College, Denmark Hill, London SE5 8BQ, **www1.salvationarmy.org.uk/history**.

APPENDIX 1

Scotland and Ireland

Scotland

The Scottish system of Poor Relief is very different to that elsewhere in the British Isles.

There is effectively a dividing line at 1845, after which poor relief became the responsibility of parochial boards set up for the purpose. Before that, it was in the hands of the church.

Before 1845, Kirk Session records and Poor Rolls are the main sources for finding names of those receiving poor relief. Most date from the 18th and 19th centuries. Records are largely at the National Archives of Scotland (NAS).

Under the 1845 Poor Law (Scotland) Act, Parochial Boards were set up to deal with poor relief. Some paupers qualified for outdoor relief, but the majority entered the poorhouse, as workhouses were known in Scotland. Often boards would come together to build poorhouses for paupers from several parishes. There was no automatic assistance available for men and women assessed as being "able-bodied poor".

Each parish kept its own general Poor Register, listing all those who received relief of any kind. Although some are now at the NAS, the majority that have survived can be located at local archives. However, up to around 1870 there is an overlap between the Kirk Session records and the Poor registers, meaning you need to check both to be thorough.

If the Poor Register hasn't survived it might be worth checking the Parochial Board minutes, although they tend not to have much information about individual paupers. Few records survive for individual poorhouses. The best you can expect to find is a register of admissions, with no real personal details, save the parish of the person admitted.

The Archives and Special Collections at the Mitchell Library in Glasgow hold more than 1,000,000 applications for poor relief made by residents of Glasgow and the West of Scotland. These records contain detailed notes and information about the applicants, their families and life. Details at

www.glasgow.gov.uk/en/Residents/Library_Services/The_Mitchell/ Archives/ poorlawarchives.htm

Ireland

The Irish Poor Law Act of 1838 introduced a system which was very similar to that in England and Wales. The island was divided into 137 Poor Law Unions which were centred around market towns where a workhouse was built with an infirmary and fever hospital attached. The management of the workhouses was the responsibility of elected Boards of Guardians with the day to day responsibility in the hands of paid officials.

The guardians were instructed to discourage all but the neediest paupers from applying to the workhouse for assistance, although it was hard to enforce this during the Great Famine.

Comprehensive records were kept, although the survival rate of admission and discharge registers is not good.

In the Republic records tend to be held by the county libraries or archives, although there are many exceptions. The National Archives of Ireland (NAI) also has a good collection, which contains material for Dublin City and County Dublin.

Material from the 27 Poor Law Unions in the North is held by the Public Record Office of Northern Ireland (PRONI).

More information can be found at **www.nationalarchives.ie/research/ poorlaw.html**

Useful Addresses

National Archives of Scotland, HM General Register House, Edinburgh EH1 3YY, tel 0131-535 1334, **www.nas.gov.uk**

National Archives of Ireland, Bishops St, Dublin 8; tel 00353-1-407 2300; **www.nationalarchives.ie.**

Public Record Office of Northern Ireland (PRONI), 66 Balmoral Ave, Belfast BT9 6NY; tel 028 9025 5905; **www.proni.gov.uk**. PRONI is moving to new premises in Belfast's Titanic Quarter in the late spring of 2011. Full details are available on its website.

APPENDIX 2

Finding Poor Law Records

Finding where Poor Law and related records are stored can be a nightmare. There are many hundreds of archives to be found across England and Wales, large and small. Details of almost all archives can be on the ARCHON database maintained by The National Archives, which will give you a contact address, a link to their website and where appropriate links to entries on the National Register of Archives.

- **www.nationalarchives.gov.uk/archon**

Most Poor Law records are kept by County Record Offices (each English county and most Welsh counties have at least one) or possibly a city archive. What each one has varies tremendously, but most are likely to have records of local government, Poor Law, Quarter Sessions, and collections of papers deposited by local charities. The best way to find out about their collections is generally from their websites. There are likely to be some references about the Poor Law and related records as they are popular research topics. A few have their own online catalogues which can be surprisingly difficult to use.

Websites also provide details of opening hours and which days of the week the record office is open. A location map and what identification is required to obtain a reader's ticket is also shown. Some County Record Offices are members of the CARN scheme where one ticket is valid in the reading rooms of each member.

Fortunately, there are several national indexes available online which can help. The easiest to use and most detailed is Access to Archives, (A2A) which contains catalogues from over 400 archives across England, allowing access to descriptions of individual items. Unfortunately it is frustratingly incomplete as the funding ended, and the project was wound up, before everything could be included. As many of the cataloguing projects were done on a regional basis, some areas are better covered than others. However, one of the most useful sources for the Old Poor Law – records of Quarter Sessions – is fully indexed:

- **www.nationalarchives.gov.uk/a2a**
- **www.archivesnetworkwales.info [the equivalent for Wales]**

The National Register of Archives (NRA) provides descriptions of collections at local record offices across England and Wales. The NRA is particularly useful if you are trying to find the records of a particular charity or philanthropist. There are also several more specialist databases describing the whereabouts of hospital records, many of which started as workhouse infirmaries.

- **www.nationalarchives.gov.uk/nra**
- **www.nationalarchives.gov.uk/hospitalrecords**

The National Archives at Kew is the most important national resource for family historians. However, there is relatively little about the Poor Law, as this was administered locally, although there is correspondence between local poor law unions and Whitehall between 1835 and 1900:

- **www.nationalarchives.gov.uk/catalogue**

There is also Global Search, which searches all the databases found on The National Archives. Unfortunately, although there are modifiers which allow you to amend your search (by date or location for example) all too often you may come up with thousands of irrelevant results. It is found at the top right side of the homepage.

- **www.nationalarchives.gov.uk**

Local studies libraries (sometimes called local history libraries or history centres) are likely to have comprehensive collections of books, including street directories. Some have archive collections as well. But their greatest asset is often a comprehensively indexed collection of press cuttings from local, and sometimes national, newspapers going back to before the First World War. These may for example include interviews with the workhouse master or former inmates and stories about the closure of "the house." They may well also have some original documents, such as poor law records or personal papers.

Local studies libraries are normally part of the central reference library, although some have been merged with the local archive service as in Gloucestershire, Hull and Norfolk. Most are listed in ARCHON (see above).

Useful addresses

The National Archives, Ruskin Avenue, Kew, Richmond TW9 4DU; tel 020-8876 3444, **www.nationalarchives.gov.uk**

Society of Genealogists, 14 Charterhouse Buildings, Goswell Road, London EC1M 7BA; tel: 020-7251 8799; **www.sog.org.uk**

Workhouse museums

There are three workhouse museums. Each one offers a different aspect of the workhouse but, with the possible exception of the smallest at Ripon, none come close to replicating what it must have been like to have been an inmate. Very little workhouse furniture survives, so visitors have to walk through bare wards and dining rooms, and it is difficult to imagine them alive with people.

Built in 1776, Gressenhall was originally a House of Industry, a proto-type workhouse which took in all the local unemployed men, women and their families. Today it houses the Norfolk Rural Life Museum.

Southwell Workhouse in Nottinghamshire (1824) was restored and re-opened by the National Trust in 2002. It is important because it was the brain-child of a local vicar and social reformer, John Becher, one of the architects behind the New Poor Law. The building clearly reflects his ideas of how paupers should be treated.

The Ripon Workhouse was opened in 1854. Here only the casual wards are open and look more or less as they did a century ago. The workhouse garden is being restored at the time of writing.

Southwell and Gressenhall both have small research study areas, staffed by knowledgeable volunteers. Although the vast majority of records relating to these unions are either at the local record office or The National Archives, they have built up some interesting collections. Both are researching inmates and workhouse staff, and welcome enquiries from people whose ancestors had a connection with the house. They are open by appointment.

Gressenhall Farm and Workhouse, Gressenhall, East Dereham NR20 3DR; tel: 01362- 860563; **www.museums.norfolk.gov.uk**

The Workhouse Museum, Allhallowgate, Ripon HG4 1LE; Tel: 01765-690799; **www.riponmuseums.co.uk**

The Workhouse, Upton Road, Southwell NG25 0PT; Tel: 01636-812250; **www.nationaltrust.org.uk/workhouse**

The workhouse at Llanfyllin in the heart of Wales has been restored in part as a community and arts centre (with an annual workhouse festival): **www.llanfyllinworkhouse.org.**

APPENDIX 3

Bibliography

There are a great many books on the Poor Law and the lives of the poor. Here is a selection which look at the national picture. In addition there are many books, booklets and articles which consider local workhouses or the relief of the poor locally. Also worth looking out for are the transcriptions of poor law records made by family history and local record societies. Most local studies libraries will have sets for their counties. Good collections for the whole country are at The National Archives and the Society of Genealogists.

Books published by the Federation of Family History Societies or Family History Partnership are on sale at **www.thefamilyhistorypartnership.com.**

Ian Anstruther, *The Scandal of Andover Workhouse* (London: Geoffrey Bles, 1973)

Brian Bailey, *Almshouses* (London: Robert Hale, 1988)

Robert Burlison, *Tracing Your Pauper Ancestors* (Pen & Sword, 2009)

Anthony Chadwick, *From Workhouse to Welfare State* (Ripon: Museum Trust, 2003 Life in the Workhouse Booklet 7)

S G and E O A Checkland (ed), *The Poor Law Report of 1834* (London: Penguin, 1974)

Kellow Chesney, *The Victorian Underworld* (London: Pelican Books, 1972)

Anne Cole, *An Introduction to Poor Law Documents before 1834* (2nd edn, Federation of Family History Societies, 1999)

Frank Crompton, *Workhouse Children* (Stroud: Sutton, 1997)

M A Crowther, *The Workhouse System 1834-1929* (London: Batsford, 1981)

Charles Dickens, 'The Wapping Workhouse' in *An Uncommercial Traveller* (London: Chapman & Hall, 1861)

Anne Digby, *Pauper Palaces* (London: Routledge and Kegan Paul, 1978)

Anne Digby, *The Poor Law in nineteenth century England and Wales* (London: Historical Association, 1982)

Felix Driver, *Power and Pauperism: the Workhouse System 1834-1884* (Cambridge: University Press, 1993)

Simon Fowler, *Workhouse: the people, the place, life behind closed doors* (The National Archives, 2007)

Jeremy Gibson et al, *Poor Law Records* (4 vols, Family History Partnership 2004-2008)

The contents of the four volumes are :

1. South-East England and East Anglia
   Covering Bedfordshire, Buckinghamshire, Cambridgeshire, Essex, Hertfordshire, Huntingdonshire, Kent, London, Middlesex, Norfolk, Suffolk, Surrey, and Sussex

2. The Midlands and Northern England
   Cheshire, Cumberland, Derbyshire, Durham, Lancashire, Leicestershire, Lincolnshire, Northamptonshire, Northumberland, Nottinghamshire, Rutland, Staffordshire, Warwickshire, Westmorland, Worcestershire, Yorkshire

3. South-West England, The Marches, and Wales
   Berkshire, Cornwall, Devon, Dorset, Gloucestershire & Bristol, Hampshire, Herefordshire, Monmouthshire, Oxfordshire, Shropshire, Somerset, Wiltshire, Worcestershire. Wales

4. Gazetteer of England and Wales
   A county-by-county listing of each poor-law union and its constituent places in England and Wales. Also useful when seeking places within civil registration and census districts

Jeremy Gibson, *Quarter Session Records for Family Historians* (The Family History Partnership, 5th edition, 2007)

David Hey (ed), *The Oxford Companion to Local and Family History* (2nd edition, Oxford University Press, 2008).

Peter Higginbotham, *The Workhouse Cookbook* (The History Press, 2008)

Michelle Higgs, *Life in the Victorian and Edwardian Workhouse* (The History Press, 2007)

Tim Hitchcock, *Down and Out in Eighteenth Century London* (London: Hambledon, 2004)

Beryl Hurley (ed), *The Handy Book of Parish Law* (Wiltshire FHS, 2000)

Steven King, *Poverty and Welfare in England 1700-1850: a regional perspective* (Manchester: University Press, 2000)

Steven King and Alannah Tomkins (eds), *The Poor in England 1700-1850: An economy of makeshifts* (Manchester: University Press, 2003)

Norman Longmate, *The Workhouse* (Pimlico, 2003)

Trevor May, *The Victorian Workhouse* (Shire, 1997)

Henry Mayhew, *London Labour and London Poor: volumes 3 and 4* (London: 1862) available online at
www.perseus.tufts.edu/cache/perscoll_bolles.html
Kathryn Morrison, *The Workhouse: A Study of Poor Law Buildings in Enland* (Swindon: English Heritage, 1999)
David Owen, *English Philanthropy, 1660-1960* (Oxford University Press, 1965)
Richard Ratcliffe, *Basic Facts about Quarter Sessions Records* (Federation of Family History Societies, 2007)
W E Tate, *The Parish Chest* (Phillimore, 1983)
John Waller, *The Real Oliver Twist: Robert Blincoe a life that illuminates a violent age* (Cambridge: Icon Books, 2005)
Peter Wood, *Poverty and the Workhouse in Victorian Britain* (Stroud: Alan Sutton, 1991)

Useful Websites - a select list

www.ancestry.co.uk/London – including poor law records for parishes and unions in the old County of London
www.nationalarchives.gov.uk/documentsonline – copies of correspondence between selected poor law unions and the authorities in London 1834-1871
www.workhouses.org.uk – superb resource and essential reference tool
www.johnh.co.uk/history/cheesmanbuilders.htm – about the builders of Brighton's first workhouse and the misconduct of the town's guardians in the 1850s
www.judandk.force9.co.uk/workhouse.html – mainly about Stratford-upon-Avon
www.kingston.gov.uk/browse/leisure/museum/kingston_history/ citizenship_in_kingston/welfare_archives.htm – examples of documents relating to Kingston almshouses and workhouse
http://www.gmcro.co.uk/cs/poor_law_records.htm – introduction to the records
www.mdlp.co.uk/resources/general/poor_law.htm – useful introduction to sme aspects of the old poor law
Indexes and databases (selection only)
www.sussexrecordsociety.org.uk/plhome.asp?an=&ap= a database to 14,000 Sussex paupers before 1834.

www.cfhs.org.uk/PoorLawPapers – index to the nearly 11,000 men and women who appeared in the settlement papers for Cambridgeshire

www.hiddenlives.org.uk – files of Children's Society about the children they helped between 1881 and 1918.

www.surreycc.gov.uk/surreyhistorycentre – admissions and discharges to and from Chertsey Workhouse

http://a-day-in-the-life.powys.org.uk/eng/social/es_compare.php – various pages relating to workhouses in Powys

www.victorianweb.org/history/poorlaw/poorlawov.html – explanatory texts on many aspects of the old and new poor laws.

www.institutions.org.uk – another general site on poor law institutions, hospitals and the like

www.historyhome.co.uk/primary.htm#poor – some key documents relating to the poor law

www.exploregenealogy.co.uk/ScotlandPoorLaw.html – introduction to the Scottish system

Appendix 4

Chronology

1563 — Justices of the Peace were authorised and empowered to raise compulsory funds for the relief of the poor and, for the first time, the poor were put into different categories.

1597 – legislation introducing the office of the Overseer of the Poor.

1601 – an Act for the Relief of the Poor (as known as the 'Elizabethan Poor Law') consolidated previous legislation regarding the poor and required that individual parishes looked after those who were unable to work.

1662 – introduction of the Settlement Laws to prevent paupers moving to parishes with more generous provision for the poor.

1698 – first workhouse built.

1782 – Gilbert's Act encouraged parishes, and groups of parishes, to build workhouses to house local poor. More than 1,000 were built.

1795 – beginnings of the Speenhamland system which saw parishes top up the earnings of unemployed or underemployed agricultural labourers.

1834 – Royal Commission on the Poor Law recommends that a network of workhouses be established across England and Wales.

1834 – Poor Law (Amendment) Act sets up 634 poor law unions each of which had to build and administer one or more workhouses.

1846 – Investigation into the abuses at Andover workhouse reveals both how badly paupers could be treated by workhouse staff and the poor state of many workhouses.

1869 – Goschen Circular (named after the President of the Poor Law Board who signed it) reminds poor law union guardians that the only assistance they can offer paupers is the workhouse.

1909 – Report of the Royal Commission on the Poor Law shows that members are split about the future administration of help for the poor, although both the majority and minority reports are agreed that poor law and workhouses should be abolished.

1929 – Poor Law Unions are abolished and their functions, including running workhouses, are passed to local authorities. Many workhouses become hospitals.

1948 – the introduction of the Welfare State finally abolishes the Poor Law. Local authority hospitals, including workhouses, are taken over by the government.

Appendix 5

Glossary

The Poor Law was refreshingly free of euphemisms and jargon. The guardians and overseers in particular liked to call a spade a spade, which occasionally may jar modern sensibilities, for example when talking about the mentally ill. However there are a few words or phrases whose meanings have either changed over the past 150 years or may not always be clear today.

Able-bodied
: Men and women between the age of 16 and 60 who judged fit enough to work for their living and there fore not to require the assistance of the poor law.

Aged
: Men and women over the age of sixty, who were too infirm to earn a living

Board
: The board of guardians which ran the local poor law union.

Casual
: A vagrant or tramp. Casual wards were where they stayed.

Deserving poor
: The Victorians generally divided the poor into the 'deserving' and the 'undeserving'. Those through no fault of their own had been reduced to poverty and who were showing, or had shown, qualities of self-help were regarded as being 'deserving' and should be looked after by charitable institutions rather than the workhouse.

Dietary
: The fixed diet proscribed for each day of the week.

Elizabeth 43
: (or the '43 of Elizabeth') The regnal year in which the original statute was passed establishing the Poor Law (1601).

Gilbert Union
: About a hundred local unions predated the New Poor Law. They were known as Gilbert Unions after an Act of 1782 which permitted their establishment. They survived after 1834 and many eventually became poor law unions.

Governor	An alternative term for the workhouse master
Guardians	Ratepayers elected to run a local poor law union
In and Outs	Paupers who regularly entered the workhouse and discharged themselves a few days or weeks after admission. They were generally very unpopular with both staff and fellow inmates.
Indoor poor	The residents of the workhouse
Indoor relief	Relief offered within the workhouse itself.
Insane	Mentally ill men and women whose condition pre vented them being looked after within the work house. Normally they were causing harm to them selves or others. Sometimes referred to as 'idiots'
Itch	Scabies - a common medical condition caused by a small parasite, similar to lice, which burrows under the skin causing severe itching. Most workhouses had specially designated "itch wards" for such cases.
"Less eligibility"	Polite term for workhouse test (which see)
Lunatic	A mental man or woman whose condition was such that they could be cared for by workhouse staff. Normally they were educationally subnormal. Some times referred to as 'imbeciles'
Oakum	Loose fibres obtained by unpicking old ropes which were then sold to ship-builders - it was mixed with tar and used for caulking (sealing the lining) of wooden ships. Picking oakum was done either using a large metal nail spike (hence the workhouse) or sometimes without tools of any kind and was very hard on the fingers.
'Offered the house'	When outdoor relief was not given, applicants could be "offered the house". As might be expected this was often not well received.
Outdoor relief	Assistance provided outside the workhouse, for example in pensions to the elderly, visits from the medical officer to the sick, and bread for the destitute. Although it was made illegal under legislation of 1834, almost all unions continued to provide it because it was both cheaper and more humane.

Overseers	Technically Overseers of the Poor. Before 1834 two ratepayers were elected by the ratepayers to look after paupers, the elderly and infirm within the parish. In larger parishes there may have been paid assistant overseers who dealt with the poor on a daily basis. The post continued until the 1880s but its importance was much reduced.
Pauper	Men and women from the lowest strata of society who could neither support themselves nor had the dignity to try to do so. Writers talked about a pauper contagion which would infect any person they came into contact with, and social a class which passed on its pauper heritage through the generations.
Poor law	The system of welfare provided by the state, either centrally or locally, for the poor.
Poor Law Union	One of 656 or so such bodies established across England and Wales after 1834 to run the workhouse and administer the poor law locally. They were managed by boards of guardians made up of elected guardians.
Public Assistance Institution	The official name given to workhouses after 1929.
Relieving officers	Employees of the union who were responsible for examining applicants for out-relief to see whether they were eligible and advising on the amount they were to be granted or whether they be offered "the house".
Settlement	The right to receive parochial assistance in the parish of the pauper's birth rather than where the individual actually lived. Much effort was expended in returning poor unfortunates to their place of birth in order to prevent them being a burden on the poor law rate payers of the parish where they lived. Although the importance of settlement faded away after 1834 it was not abolished until 1946.
Skilly	A thin oatmeal or gruel provided at breakfast or for supper.

Spike	Nickname for a workhouse, by implication transferred to any low dosshouse or place occupied by vagrants or tramps.
Task	The work undertaken by able-bodied paupers or casuals. In theory it was meant to contribute towards the expenses of their keep, but often it was just work performed for the sake of it.
'The House'	A term for the workhouse.
Undeserving poor	Those who did not wish to save themselves from poverty or deprivation; who sponged off charities and the poor law.
Union	The shorthand term often used to describe a Poor Law Union.
Vestry	The body elected by the ratepayers which was the local government authority in parishes before the introduction of district, borough and county councils in the 1880s and 1890s.
Workhouse test	The principle that conditions in the workhouse should never be better than those of "an independent labourer of the lowest class."